T0125702

HAN IN THE UPPER LEFT:

A Brief History of Korean Americans in the Pacific Northwest

Printed in Canada by Imprimerie Gauvin

Publisher:
Chin Music Press
1501 Pike Place #329
Seattle, WA 98101
www.chinmusicpress.com

HAN IN THE UPPER LEFT:

A Brief History of Korean Americans in the Pacific Northwest

Spring 2015
Korean American Historical Society
Chin Music Press

CHIN MUSIC
P   R   E   S   S

TABLE OF CONTENTS

INTRODUCTION

We Koreans believe that we are a people defined by *han*, a collective sense of suffering, oppression, and hardship. After generations of wars and colonialism on the Korean Peninsula, we are a people who are haunted and driven by the past, even as we forge ahead to build new histories in Korea and around the world, including in the upper left corner of the continental United States.[1] Without attempting to be comprehensive, this book is a modest effort to capture some of our stories in Seattle and its surrounding areas, with an eye toward conveying to ourselves and to our friends and neighbors in the Pacific Northwest who we are and who we might become. Reflective of our varied and complex histories, we have many, many different stories to tell. We offer here only glimpses into our past and our present, but we hope they will encourage our readers to share their own memories with their families and our communities.

Our story is rooted in Korea. Korean Americans' ties to Korea have significantly shaped the ways in which we have developed our identities and social institutions. Since the dawn of the twentieth century, Koreans in Hawai'i and North America have maintained transpacific connections, with some returning to Korea and others sending for "picture brides" to join them on the other side of the world. In the 1920s and 1930s, the movement for Korean independence from Japanese colonialism involved nearly every Korean in the United States and formed the foundation around which Korean American political, religious, and social life revolved. Their adamant affirmation of their Korean identity—and their rejection of their status as colonial Japanese subjects— drove Korean Americans to struggle for something better in the United States, a place mythologized as the land of oppor-

---

1 We borrow the phrase "upper left" from Blue Scholars, the dynamic hip hop duo representing the Pacific Northwest in the most lyrical and radical ways possible.

tunity and freedom but experienced on the ground as the land of white supremacy and daily exploitation.

Many Korean Americans know little of that history these days, but our lives are no less shaped by its ongoing effects and legacies. Although individual stories point to a wide array of personal motivations, US ties to Korea—political, cultural, economic, and military—have been the driving force behind mass migrations of Koreans since the beginning of the Korean War. Call it the US empire or something else, but US influence over Korea is undeniably the global context in which millions of Koreans have made the United States home over the last half century. Korean Americans today are incredibly heterogeneous. Some of us landed recently at the Seattle-Tacoma International Airport, with all of our worldly possessions and grand dreams of a better future, while others have been in the United States for generations. Many of us identify as Christians, even if that might not have been the case back in Korea. We are also Buddhists and atheists. We are professionals—doctors, lawyers, real estate agents. We are workers—janitors, waiters, retail clerks. We are small business owners, working incredibly long hours in neighborhood shops and restaurants. We are God-fearing social conservatives. We are fearless activists, carrying on a radical tradition very much alive on the Korean Peninsula. We are all these things, and much more.

Han in the Upper Left explores the multiple and varied ways that Koreans have established communities in the Pacific Northwest, particularly in and around Seattle, Washington. By "communities," we mean the creative ways and processes that human beings cultivate a collective sense of belonging, on the level of families, organizations, and historical consciousness. We emphatically do not mean "assimilation" into American society, for such a framing homogenizes Korean Americans—and all "immigrants"—and naturalizes the United States as somehow universally welcoming across time and space. We know that has never been the case for Koreans or for anyone racialized as not white. Approaching our histories in the Pacific Northwest locally and globally, we seek to demonstrate the variety of methods and strategies that Korean Americans have employed to pursue what it means to be Korean American. That variety, we argue, reflects and encompasses a complex history of US-Korean relations and Korean struggles for self-determination, in our ancestral homeland and in the United States. Through this slim volume, we hope to reveal some of the many tensions and contradictions born out of that history.

Gloria Lee (center) with two friends at a Korean community picnic, Lincoln Park, 1974. Courtesy of Mansop Hahn.

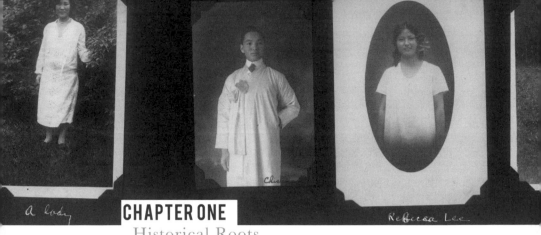

a lady

Rebecca Lee

CHAPTER ONE
Historical Roots

Empire has deeply influenced Korean lives in the United States, as Japan and the United States have laid claims over East Asia and the Pacific since the second half of the nineteenth century. Driven out of their homeland by Japanese colonialism and recruited and drawn to lands occupied by the United States—Hawai'i and then the mainland—early Korean migrants encountered displacement and hostility on both sides of the Pacific. Legally categorized as "Japanese subjects," Koreans found themselves in a racially segregated world in the United States, restricted to certain neighborhoods and jobs—primarily in agriculture and domestic service—and often confused and classified with other Asians. In between these restrictions and demands, and regardless of their relatively small numbers, Koreans created spaces for full and meaningful lives, striving for better opportunities and building families and communities, wherever and however they could.

Migrant Laborers and Picture Brides, 1890s–1920s

Korean migrants moved to the Pacific Northwest as workers in the early decades of the twentieth century, joining a circuit of migrant labor up and down the Pacific coast—from the salmon canneries in Alaska to the agricultural fields of Washington, Oregon, and California. Despite laws prohibiting "aliens ineligible to citizenship" from owning real property, some Korean migrants were able to buy land by forming multi-family collectives. Not all Koreans were manual workers, though. Overcoming US exclusion laws and Japanese colonial policies in Korea, small numbers of students, political refugees, and picture brides entered the United States before World War II.

One of the first Koreans in the Pacific Northwest was Ji In Hong. In 1898, he left Korea to try gold prospecting in Canada's Yukon Territory, landing first on the US mainland and making his way north to Alaska. Prevented from entering Canada, Hong stayed on in Alaska and worked as a packer for prospectors in Skagway. When the gold-rush traffic through Skagway slowed down at the turn of the century, Hong moved to Ketchikan and became a successful businessman, returning to Korea to marry and stopping for a time in Hawai'i with his family. Moving between Korea, Hawai'i, Alaska, and the ports of San Francisco and Seattle, Hong traversed many of the routes that Korean migrants would take as they sought jobs and formed families and communities across the Pacific.[1]

Hong had left Korea at a moment of great transformation. Korea's status as the "Hermit Kingdom" was under attack in the second half of the nineteenth century, as the United States, Japan, and other imperial powers vied for influence over the peninsula. In spring 1871, the US government dispatched to Korea a fleet of five heavily armed US Navy ships, with 1,230 men aboard, ostensibly to negotiate a treaty to protect shipwrecked American sailors. The US Navy soon provoked a bloody battle with Korean forces, killing at least 250 Koreans, seizing five forts, and ransacking and burning nearby villages. The United States compelled the Chosŏn Dynasty to sign a commercial treaty in 1882. In the meantime, a group of American sugar plantation owners steered the Hawaiian Kingdom toward US markets and eventually US annexation in 1898, firmly placing Hawai'i in the orbit of the American empire.[2]

---

1 Joe Hong, "Oral History: An Interview with Joe Hong," *Occasional Papers of the Korean American Historical Society* 1 (1985): 42-53.

2 Moon-Ho Jung, "Seditious Subjects: Race, State Violence, and the U.S. Empire," *Journal of Asian American Studies* 14, no. 2 (June 2011): 228-231.

Joseph Hong (third on right), son of Ji In Hong, University of Alaska ROTC, 1940. Courtesy of Mike Hagiwara.

It was in that global context of empire that a handful of Korean students, merchants, diplomats, and laborers entered the United States in the late nineteenth century, followed by a greater number of workers bound for Hawai'i beginning in 1902. Having recruited Chinese and then increasingly Japanese workers, Hawaii's sugar plantation owners anxiously turned to Korea to offset the growing militancy of the local labor movement. Horace Allen, a US missionary who had become a close confidant of King Kojong in Seoul, represented the plantation owners and convinced the Korean monarch to allow his subjects to migrate to Hawai'i. Provided with passports and monetary loans by the Korean government, 7,226 Korean migrants arrived in Hawai'i between 1903 and 1905. A smaller group of approximately one thousand Koreans was recruited around the same time to work on Mexico's henequen plantations.[3]

---

3 Bong-youn Choy, *Koreans in America* (Chicago: Nelson-Hall, 1979), chapter 4; Lee Houchins and Chang-su Houchins, "The Korean Experience in America, 1903-1924," *Pacific Historical Review* 43, no. 4 (November 1974): 548-555; Sucheng Chan, "Introduction" to Mary Paik Lee, *A Quiet Odyssey: A Pioneer Korean Woman in America* (Seattle: University of Washington Press, 1990), xxxix.

Shifting power struggles over the Korean Peninsula continued to open and close migration routes. With its victories in the First Sino-Japanese War (1894–1895) and the Russo-Japanese War (1904–1905)—both fought on Korean soil—Japan emerged as an imperial power that the West could not ignore. While hosting and facilitating the negotiations between Russia and Japan that would conclude with the Treaty of Portsmouth (1905), US officials agreed separately with Japanese officials to recognize Japanese control over Korea in exchange for Japanese recognition of US rule in the Philippines. The Japanese government quickly took steps to rule over Korea more formally, prohibiting the emigration of Koreans abroad and then annexing the peninsula outright in 1910. Fully aware of these developments, Koreans abroad felt attached to their homeland more than ever, even as many of them moved farther away physically to the US mainland.[4]

In search of a better life beyond plantation labor in Hawai'i, many Koreans moved to the western United States, where, as in Hawai'i, they found themselves subjected to a legal and socioeconomic regime rooted in white supremacy. Like the Chinese and Japanese before them, Koreans were largely restricted to agriculture, mining, and railroad construction in rural areas and service jobs in urban areas like Seattle and San Francisco. Some Koreans found work on the Great Northern Railway, settling down in Western Washington—especially Seattle, the railroad's western terminus—or moving onto the farmlands of Oregon, California, Colorado, Utah, Kansas, and Montana.[5] Other Koreans, particularly unmarried men, joined a circuit of seasonal migrant labor that Chinese, Japanese, and Filipino workers traveled every year. They sailed to Alaska in the summer months to work in the salmon canneries before returning to Seattle or San Francisco, bases from

---

4 Sucheng Chan, *Asian Americans: An Interpretive History* (New York: Twayne, 1991), 3-23.

5 Houchins and Houchins, "The Korean Experience," 555.

which they would find work harvesting fruits and vegetables along the West Coast. Between jobs many would congregate in hotels and gambling houses in Seattle's International District. Some of the Korean cannery workers were also college students, who earned money for tuition and books by working summer canning seasons in Alaska.[6]

The number of Korean women in the United States increased in the second decade of the twentieth century, with most of them entering as picture brides. Hoping to curb anti-Japanese sentiments among Koreans abroad, the Japanese state allowed nearly a thousand Korean women—who agreed through intermediaries and photographs to marry men in the United States— to move to the United States between 1910 and 1924. Drawn to marriage as a possible route to education, travel, and adventure, most of these young women did not find the kind of liberation that they had hoped for. The lives of Korean women proved particularly strenuous, as childcare and housework did not relieve them from wage work outside the home.[7]

Early Korean Women's Stories

As a young teenager in southeastern Korea, In-Sook longed for an independent life away from her restrictive home village. On her fifteenth birthday, she ran away to Busan, where a matchmaker helped her exchange photographs with Korean men in the United States and select a husband. Because her future husband was unable to send for her immediately, In-Sook was forced to move back home, where her family subjected her to

---

6 Jay Kun Yoo, *The Koreans in Seattle* (Elkins Park, PA: Philip Jaisohn Memorial Foundation, 1979), chapter 1; "Filipino Cannery Unionism Across Three Generations, 1930s-1980s," Seattle Civil Rights and Labor History Project, http:// depts.washington.edu/civilr/Cannery intro.htm; and Lee Chang Hei, "Korean Network in Washington State," *Korea Times*, January 1, 1978 (translated by Chong Eun Ahn).

7 Sonia Sunoo, "Korean Women Pioneers of the Pacific Northwest," *Oregon Historical Quarterly* 79, no. 1 (Spring 1978): 51-63.

abuse and humiliation for "selling herself." She secretly made arrangements to stay at her in-laws' home until her husband had saved enough money for her passage. When her father-in-law passed away unexpectedly, In-Sook, as the eldest daughter-in-law, was forced to remain in Korea for a traditional mourning period of three years. At the age of twenty, she finally joined her husband in the United States. To commemorate her newfound freedom, In-Sook pulled the white mourning ribbon out of her hair and threw it into the ocean as her ship pulled away toward Seattle. She moved to Montana, where she and her husband operated a sugar beet farm and raised ten children. After her husband's death, In-Sook continued to run the farm on her own, she claimed proudly, without ever asking "not for even one slice of stale bread from anyone."[8]

Over her family's objections, seventeen-year-old Myong-Soon decided to marry a Korean man living in the United States and left Korea in 1914. Once she arrived in Seattle, a group of thirty Korean bachelors, who worked seasonally in Alaska, organized a wedding celebration before the newlyweds left for the husband's farm in Montana. Myong-Soon's husband had moved from Korea to Hawai'i to work on a sugar plantation, but soon left for the mainland. Together with four friends, he collectively leased land in Montana, where a Korean farming community was taking root. By the time Myong-Soon arrived, there were nearly four hundred Koreans living in the area. Koreans in Montana formed a close-knit community, she would recall later, particularly the Friendship Club (*Chinmock-hoe*) that women organized to facilitate communal gatherings.

Other Korean women remembered a more arduous life shaped by racial discrimination, social isolation, and daily hardship. Eighteen-year-old Soon-Hi left Korea dreaming

---

8 The following stories of In-Sook, Myong-Soon, and Soon-Hi are from Sunoo, "Korean Women Pioneers." Sunoo does not include the women's last names.

Picture Bride Shin-Sook Kim and her husband Chu Woon Kim work on a farm in Montana. Courtesy of the Shin-Sook Kim Collection.

of an easier life and, like Myong-Soon, met her husband in Seattle before moving to Montana to begin truck farming. Soon-Hi and her husband toiled in the fields every day, growing vegetables for nearly a quarter century, and struggled to raise seven children. Soon-Hi's husband died when she was pregnant with their seventh child. Looking back on her life of hard work, she remarked, "Even the life of a butcher in Korea would have been better!" Although work defined and, in many cases, dominated Korean migrants' lives, they found hope and sustenance in their families and communities. For many, they also found hope through a political commitment to Korean independence from Japanese colonialism.

Forging a Korean American Identity
The Korean population in the continental United States was relatively small before the 1960s, due in no small measure to restrictions and prohibitions placed on migration by the Japanese colonial regime and US immigration laws. The 1910 census listed only one Korean in the Seattle area, a number that grew to thirty-seven by 1920. Across the US mainland, there were 1,677 Koreans in 1920 and 1,711 in 1940.[9] The low numbers, however, do not mean that Koreans were historically insignificant. Koreans in the United States built vibrant communities to protect themselves against labor exploitation, anti-Asian laws, and racial violence. Mutual aid and political societies as well as Christian churches served as support networks for Korean workers in the face of white supremacy. Perhaps most significantly, the struggle against Japanese colonialism gave Koreans in the United States—and, really, Koreans worldwide—a shared political identity, a communal sense of belonging to a wider cause.

Koreans in the United States encountered a barrage of anti-Asian laws and practices. From the Chinese Exclusion Act (1882) to the 1924 Immigration Act, the US federal government systematically restricted and prohibited the immigration and naturalization of Asians. The 1924 law prohibited the entry of "aliens ineligible to citizenship," a racialized and racializing status that Koreans shared with other Asians. The 1790 Naturalization Act had restricted to "free white persons" the right of naturalized citizenship, which was extended to persons of African descent in 1870 but not to all persons without regard to race until 1952. Beginning in 1913, Koreans living in California and then in Washington, Oregon, Idaho, and many other states were likewise subjected to state laws prohibiting "aliens ineligible to

---

9 Ronald Takaki, *Strangers from a Different Shore: A History of Asian Americans* (Boston: Little, Brown and Company, 1989), 270; "Korean Americans in King County," Historylink essay, http://www.historylink.org/index.cfm?DisplayPage=output.cfm&File Id=3251.

citizenship" from owning land or leasing land for longer than three years. Combined with daily acts of hostility and violence, these laws effectively made Koreans and other Asians perpetual aliens in the supposed "land of immigrants." Though in demand as migrant workers, they were viewed and treated as persons unfit to become full-fledged "Americans."[10]

These contradictions shaped Korean migrants' everyday lives. In 1913, when eleven Korean workers recruited to pick apricots arrived in the Hemet Valley in Southern California, an angry white mob greeted them and forced them back on the train to Los Angeles. No doubt offended by the violent welcome, the Korean workers became incensed when the mob assumed that they were Japanese. The Japanese consulate's offer to intervene in the affair intensified their ire. In support of the workers, the Southern California chapter of the Korean National Association wired the US Secretary of State to ask that the matter be dropped rather than negotiated through the Japanese government.[11] Simultaneously subjected to white supremacy and Japanese colonialism, these workers fervently claimed their own identity as Koreans.

The Korean National Association was a distinct outgrowth of Korean migrants' political organizing. Soon after their arrival, Korean workers in Hawai'i had formed village councils, or *dong-hoe*, which functioned as mutual aid societies and representative bodies from the various plantations. In 1907, the councils were unified as the United Korean Society, or *Hanin Hapsong Hyop-hoe*, which eventually evolved into the Korean National Association (KNA) in 1909. Headquartered in San Francisco, the

---

10   Chan, *Asian Americans*, 47. For more on Washington's Alien Land Law and the repeal struggle, see Nicole Grant, "White Supremacy and the Alien Land Laws of Washington State" (2008), Seattle Civil Rights and Labor History Project, http://depts.washington.edu/civilr/alien land laws.htm.

11   Linda Shin, "Koreans in America, 1903-1945," in *Roots: An Asian American Reader*, edited by Amy Tachiki et al. (Los Angeles: UCLA Asian American Studies Center, 1971), 200-206.

KNA served a number of roles for Korean Americans, sponsoring political refugees from Korea, publishing a newspaper, helping to locate jobs, and raising funds for the independent Korean provisional government-in-exile in Shanghai. In many ways the KNA acted as the de facto representative for Koreans living in the United States. From Hawai'i and Seattle to Chicago and New York, Koreans established organizations for Korean independence, including the Seattle-based *Sinhung Tongmang-hoe.*[12]

Learning of Japan's formal annexation of Korea in 1910 deepened Korean Americans' commitment to national independence. With annexation emerged a colonial regime determined to regulate Korean lives and to suppress anticolonial activities. Japanese was made the official language of instruction in Korean schools, with teachers from Japan replacing Korean teachers. The Japanese state also prohibited the assembly of more than three Koreans, closed down Korean newspapers, placed restrictions on Buddhist temples and Christian churches, and remapped Korea's landscape with Japanese names. Koreans endured separate and unequal treatment, subjected to an array of laws, policies, and violence tightly controlled by the colonial state.[13] Challenging the Japanese empire defined Korean communities and helped to unify them in Korea and around the world.

The struggle for Korean independence also generated tensions and divisions within Korean communities in the United States. Park Yong-man led a faction committed to militant radicalism, in contrast to Syngman Rhee's insistence on lobbying and diplomacy. Ahn Ch'ang-ho, in the meantime, appealed for mutual aid and self-help among Koreans. These leaders and their organizations pursued multiple strategies, from diplomatic entreaties and petitions to international peace conferences and the establishment of military training centers in the United

---

12 Choy, *Koreans in America*, 100; Takaki, *Strangers from a Different Shore*, 280.

13 Chan, "Introduction"; Michael E. Robinson, *Korea's Twentieth-Century Odyssey: A Short History* (Honolulu: University of Hawai'i Press, 2007), chapter 2.

States and Manchuria. Some Koreans living in the United States embraced direct action, as when Chang In-whan assassinated Durham Stevens, an American hired by the Japanese state to drum up support for Japanese policies in Korea. Chang's impassioned act on the streets of San Francisco in 1908 mobilized Koreans across the United States to come to his defense.[14]

Eleven years later, the March 1st Movement in Korea gripped the attention of Koreans worldwide. Inspired by Woodrow Wilson's call for national self-determination and drawing from a long history of political organizing, radical students in Korea joined Christian and Buddhist leaders to draft a declaration of Korean national autonomy and to call for a day of mass protest to commemorate the death of King Kojong. Nearly a million Koreans took part in the March 1st uprising, and spontaneous marches and protests persisted through the summer. Taken by surprise at the strength and size of the movement, the Japanese colonial police exerted brutal force to suppress it. Korean historians estimate that the reactionary campaign resulted in more than 7,500 deaths and 12,522 arrests.[15]

The March 1st Movement spurred nationalist activities among Koreans in the United States. Nearly all of them got involved in some way in the movement to oust Japan from the peninsula. Nearly every single Korean resident in the United States, even the poorest agricultural workers, made an average contribution of thirty dollars, about one month's income, to Korean independence between March 1919 and December 1920. Although Koreans continued to be divided on the best strategies to advance independence, they came together as Koreans, cultivating a shared sense of belonging in a place far removed from their homeland. Living outside the reach of the Japanese colonial police,

---

14 Choy, *Koreans in America*, chapter 8.

15 Robinson, *Korea's Twentieth-Century Odyssey*, 47-49.

Koreans in America helped to sustain the broader antico-lonial movement.[16]

The independence movement, in turn, opened up social and political spaces to address other issues. Though outnumbered demographically, Korean women became integral to political organizing. They formed the Korean Women's Association in Sacramento, California, in 1917 to aid the KNA's activities and to organize boycotts of Japanese goods. In 1919, a number of Korean women's political organizations merged into the Korean Women's Patriotic League, which focused on raising funds for the government-in-exile, boycotting Japanese products, and promoting educational and relief work in both the United States and Korea.[17] Sung-Hark (Lee) Kang, who had moved from Busan to Hawai'i in 1917 and later to Oregon, served as the secretary of the Korean Women's Relief Society of Hawai'i. The society engaged in a host of activities on behalf of Korean independence. "When Mr. Ch'ang-ho Ahn died, we sent off fundraising letters and went around every day to collect donations for the independence movement," Kang recalled. "We used to also work for Dr. Rhee whenever he came on tour to lecture or attend conventions. We used to also put on a lot of plays. . . . We did a show in Honolulu and collected some money, and we went around to all the regions to put on shows and made money and sent it all off to the government-in-exile in Shanghai."[18]

For Koreans in the United States, maintaining their Korean language and identity had a political purpose—it was a critical means to foster a historical consciousness and to create a sense of community. Korean parents' desire to pass on the language to

---

16 Figure is from Choy, *Koreans in America*, 158. See also Chan, *Asian Americans*, 98-99.

17 Choy, *Koreans in America*, 119.

18 "The Kang Family: An Oral History of First and Second Generation Korean Americans in the Early 1900s," *Occasional Papers of the Korean American Historical Society* 2 (1996): 32-33.

Korean Women's Relief Society of Hawai'i (established 1919) stage a play to raise funds for Korean independence. Courtesy of the Sung Hark Kang collection.

the next generation emerged within that context. Myong-Soon, the Korean picture bride who moved to a close-knit Korean farming community in Montana, and fellow Korean mothers nearby attempted to organize Korean language schools on numerous occasions. Although farm work often took precedence, these Korean women never forgot where they came from to forge a Korean identity in rural Montana.[19] For generations of Korean Americans, being and becoming Korean meant a resolute commitment to fighting Japanese colonial rule.

Anticolonial work also placed Christian churches at the center of Korean American communities. Many Korean migrants had converted to Christianity in Korea under the tutelage of Western missionaries, who first arrived in Korea in the nineteenth century. American Protestants like Horace Allen came to play an influential role in Korean society and helped to recruit a high

---

19 Sunoo, "Korean Women Pioneers," 57. See also Takaki, *Strangers from a Different Shore*, 279.

proportion of Christians (nearly 40 percent) to Hawai'i.[20] Christianity opened up opportunities for Korean converts, especially women, as it enabled them to learn to read and write and to participate in public activities that the Chosŏn Dynasty restricted to men. Barred from inheriting property, traveling outdoors in the daytime, or obtaining higher education, Korean women found Christian missionary schools, including Ewha University, to be an invaluable sanctuary in an increasingly patriarchal order.[21]

While many women experienced Christianity as a means for their own liberation, Koreans in general came to see Christianity as a central resource for the Korean independence movement. Because the Japanese colonial project did not rest on or affiliate with Christianity, Koreans did not identify Christianity with imperialism, in contrast to peoples in many parts of the world. Indeed, the prominence of Korean Christian leaders in the March 1st Movement—and Protestant missionaries' provision of refuge and aid to nationalist activists—concretized Christianity as a potentially anticolonial institution on the Korean Peninsula. That the Japanese state specifically targeted Christians in suppressing the March 1st Movement only magnified that political and cultural association of Christianity and anticolonial politics in Korea and in the United States.[22]

Koreans embraced and pursued this religious and political connection in Hawai'i and on the West Coast. The earliest migrants established the first Korean churches on the sugar plantations of Hawai'i within six months of their arrival. In the early decades of the twentieth century, Korean American churches served multiple purposes, functioning as centers of worship, education, and anti-Japanese politics. Many churches offered Korean and English language classes to Korean workers and their

---

20 Chan, "Introduction," xli; Takaki, *Strangers from a Different Shore*, 278-279.

21 Chan, "Introduction," xxxvi-xxxix.

22 Chan, "Introduction," xxx and xxxi.

families and worked closely with the KNA and other organizations to advance the cause of Korean independence. Serving as meeting places for weekly worship services, political discussions, and fundraising events, churches became the hub of Korean American life.[23]

From Korea to Hawai'i to the Pacific Northwest

The experiences of Korean Americans who ended up in Gresham, Oregon, in the 1940s illustrate the historical themes discussed above—empire, migrant labor, white supremacy, gender, nationalist politics, community, and identity. Initially recruited to Hawai'i as plantation workers, a group of thirty-three Korean men decided collectively to seek a better life on the mainland. Sometime between 1905 and 1912, they left plantation labor behind and secured jobs in railroad work in Montana through Japanese labor contractors in San Francisco. Once in Montana and earning less than they felt they deserved, these Korean workers attempted to move to the Chinese laborers' railroad camp, where the wages were higher. The railroad company stopped them en route and established a segregated Korean camp to keep their wages low. Once the rail line was completed, Korean workers dispersed in smaller groups, some to the agricultural fields of Idaho and others to Butte, Montana, a city with an established Chinatown that provided relative safety to generations of Chinese, Japanese, and Korean workers.[24]

Although some of these Korean men soon left Butte for work in Alaska's fish canneries or journeyed farther east, most stayed to farm in Montana. Hoping to move beyond a life of migrant labor, many married picture brides from Korea and began putting down roots. They spent most of their time out on the field with their

---

23 Takaki, *Strangers from a Different Shore*, 278; Houchins and Houchins, "Korean Experience," 564–565; Chan, *Asian Americans*, 74.

24 For the Butte/Gresham farming community, see Kyung Sook Cho Gregor, "Korean Immigrants in Gresham, Oregon: Community Life and Social Adjustment" (M.A. thesis, University of Oregon, 1963).

wives and children, specializing in the cultivation of potatoes, radishes, green onions, and sugar beets. But they also expressed a desire to forge a Korean identity and community. Korean families in rural Montana hired a Korean student to conduct Korean language classes for their children; a Korean Christian minister occasionally stopped over to lead them in worship service. Korean farmers were also attuned to the movement for Korean independence, subscribing to the KNA's weekly newspaper and sending donations to the exile government in Shanghai.

Soon-Hi, one of the picture brides who moved to Montana, was a part of this Korean community. After her husband's death, Soon-Hi was convinced by her son, a shipyard welder in Oregon, that she should join him there. The bombing of Pearl Harbor precipitated her decision to move. Korean families felt the impact of anti-Japanese hostility in Montana as local landowners and merchants began to refuse to lease land or extend credit to Korean families. In the meantime, the expulsion and incarceration of Japanese Americans from western Oregon (and California and Washington) generated a great demand for farmworkers near Portland. On her family's move westward, Soon-Hi recalled, hotels and restaurants refused them service. Other Korean families in Butte soon followed her family's lead by moving to Gresham, Oregon. A Korean community of five or six families, spanning three generations, took root there. With legal decisions overturning alien land laws, these Korean families began buying land after World War II. By the 1960s, they collectively owned 262 acres, the largest landholding held by Korean Americans outside of California.[25]

Though not representative of all Koreans in the United States, the experiences of Korean Americans in Gresham illustrate the kind of hard labor that Korean migrants endured and the vibrancy of the identity and community that they built. Sung-Hark (Lee) Kang and her children moved to Gresham in 1950, drawn there

---

25 For Soon-Hi's story, see Sunoo, "Korean Women Pioneers," 58-60.

by what she had seen on a visit shortly after World War II. She recalled:

> There were a lot of Koreans living in Gresham at that time. After the year's harvest was all in, they'd make rice cakes and sweet liquors to share with each other, just like in a Korean farm village, and they'd go around from house to house and meet to visit and socialize. It all looked so nice and heartwarming to me. Seeing them live so warmly with each other even though outside, the snow was piled up like mountains, I decided that I'd gather all my children and make a place for myself there.[26]

Kang felt a bond with the Korean community in Gresham because she had lived through the same historical experiences as her new neighbors had. She had left Busan for Hawai'i decades earlier to marry Chi Kwon Kang, a plantation laborer from Seoul. Although her children initially had a difficult time adjusting to the rigors of agricultural labor, they eventually found their way. In the Pacific Northwest, the Kang family, like many other Koreans, found something that they had been searching for: home.[27]

---

26 "The Kang Family," 31.

27 "The Kang Family," 62-63.

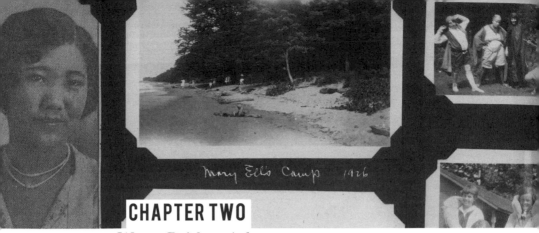

Mary Eil's Camp 1926

CHAPTER TWO

Wars, Brides, Adoptees

The end of World War II and the eruption of the Korean War deepened ties between the United States and Korea and initiated a new wave of migrations across the Pacific. As Korea assumed a new pivotal role in global geopolitics, the United States deployed military personnel and arms to the Korean Peninsula on a scale unimaginable just years earlier. US military intervention in Korea and, more generally, in East Asia facilitated the formation of interracial families and the migration of Korean military brides and adoptees to the United States. Many ended up in the Pacific Northwest, as Korean women accompanied their spouses to Fort Lewis near Tacoma, Washington, and the largest Korean adoption agency directed Korean children to families near its headquarters in Oregon. Although the rising US influence over Korea drove the new wave of migration as before, military brides and adoptees often found themselves isolated from or ostracized by fellow Korean Americans. They, in turn, formed their own organizations to build a sense of community and identity in a land where white supremacy, even if disavowed, remained the norm.

Race and Wars for Liberation

World War II posed a series of contradictions for Korean Americans. Particularly after the United States entered the war, Korean Americans saw the promise of Korea's liberation from Japanese colonial rule and lent their support to the US war effort. At the same time, they witnessed and experienced a surge in anti-Japanese (and anti-Asian) sentiments and policies in the United States. Korean families like Soon-Hi's, who took over agricultural jobs and farms held by Japanese Americans before their mass expulsion and incarceration, encountered angry white neighbors who shouted at them, "Japs go home!" Because Koreans were formally classified as subjects of Japan before and during World War II, they fell under the category of "enemy aliens" after Pearl Harbor. Koreans living in Hawai'i were subjected to martial law and encountered severe restrictions on their physical movement and financial transactions. The Korean National Association (KNA) advised all Korean Americans to wear badges identifying themselves as Korean, not Japanese, "for security purposes" and strove to revoke the status of Koreans as "Japanese nationals" and "enemy aliens."[1]

The daily humiliation of being mistaken for Japanese, compounded by the racist venom behind that misidentification, did not check Korean Americans' involvement in the US war drive. Many Koreans had language skills prized by the US military, which employed them as Japanese language translators and propaganda broadcasters. Notable Korean American scholars—like Bong-youn Choy at the University of California, Berkeley, and Harold Sunoo at the University of Washington—were recruited to teach college extension classes on Japanese and Korean politics, language, and culture to US soldiers. Some Koreans also served as translators in US concentration camps, while others explicitly refused to do so. Even if not directly working in service to the US military, Korean Americans responded enthusiastically to the war effort. Between 1942 and 1943, the small population of ten thousand Korean

---

1 Ronald Takaki, *Strangers from a Different Shore: A History of Asian Americans* (Boston: Little, Brown and Company, 1989), 264, 365; Bong-youn Choy, *Koreans in America* (Chicago: Nelson-Hall, 1979), 173; Wayne Patterson, *The Ilse: First-Generation Korean Immigrants in Hawai'i, 1903-1973* (Honolulu: University of Hawai'i Press, 2000), 179-183.

Americans purchased more than $239,000 worth of defense bonds.[2]

Korean national liberation at the conclusion of World War II proved illusory. The Allied forces' victory spelled the end of Japanese colonialism on the Korean Peninsula, but the jubilation Koreans felt turned to confusion and division as the major powers placed Korea under "Allied trusteeship." Fearing the Soviet Union's growing influence, US officials hastily divided the peninsula at the thirty-eighth parallel and began the military occupation of the southern half. By 1948, the Soviet Union and the United States had facilitated the materialization of two profoundly different states in Korea, with people's committees and communists controlling the northern half and a right-wing regime under Syngman Rhee ruling the south. Both states showed a determination to try to unify an independent Korea, engaging in military skirmishes until North Korea launched a full-scale invasion on June 25, 1950. The Korean War (1950–1953) was a civil war in the context of the larger Cold War, in which the United States (under the banner of the United Nations), the Soviet Union, and the People's Republic of China fought for supremacy over East Asia and the world.[3]

The unprecedented scale of violence devastated Korea for generations. A symptom and a cause of the massive arms race between the United States and the Soviet Union, the Korean War saw the first extensive use of jet aircraft and napalm, weapons that killed the civilian population en masse and annihilated Korea's landscape. Between 1950 and 1953, US bombers

---

2 Choy, *Koreans in America,* 173; Takaki, *Strangers from a Different Shore,* 363-367; Mel Kang, Korean American Historical Society Oral History Project (KAHS Oral History), interview with Sun-Hee Yoon, Moon-Ho Jung, and Hwasook Nam, Seattle, Washington, May 22, 2009. Kang recalls that his mother refused to serve as an interpreter for her interned neighbors.

3 Bruce Cumings, *The Korean War* (New York: Modern Library, 2010); Kim Hyŏngsik and Kim Boonhi, KAHS Oral History Project, interview with Sun-Hee Yoon, Seattle, Washington, April 21, 2009.

dropped tens of thousands of tons of napalm, the incendiary US Army trade journals termed a "wonder" and a "blazing success." An American general ordered thousand-pound versions of napalm bombs that could "wipe out all life in [a] tactical locality," an approach that destroyed entire peasant villages. It is estimated that at least two million civilians were killed in the course of the war, a higher civilian death ratio than that of either World War II or the Vietnam War. By 1951, five million Koreans had become displaced refugees, as desperate families fled the shifting front line. US bombing raids destroyed almost all of the major cities and agriculture-producing areas in North Korea.[4]

The Korean War killed and displaced millions of Koreans, including these women and children in Seoul, November 1, 1950. Courtesy of the Department of Defense. Photograph by Captain F. L. Scheiber.

4 See Sahr Conway-Lanz, "Beyond No Gun Ri: Refugees and the United States Military in the Korean War," *Diplomatic History* 29, no. 1 (January 2005):49-81; Bruce Cumings, *The Origins of the Korean War: The Roaring of the Cataract, 1947-1950, vol. II* (Princeton: Princeton University Press, 1990); Cumings, *The Korean War*; Charles J. Hanley, Sang-Hun Choe, and Martha Mendoza, *The Bridge at No Gun Ri: A Hidden Nightmare from the Korean War* (New York: Henry Holt, 2001).

The signing of the armistice on July 27, 1953, left behind two Koreas in ruins, geopolitically divided and, though formally independent, practically dependent on global powers invested in fighting the Cold War in and through Korea. The United States continued to support Rhee's anticommunist and antidemocratic regime, establishing a number of military bases across South Korea. The movement of US troops to Korea before, during, and after the Korean War sparked a new wave of Korean migrations to the United States, beginning with Korean women married to US military personnel and Korean children adopted by American families. These new migrants would dramatically increase the number of Korean Americans in the Pacific Northwest and in the United States, where anticommunism enabled and indeed demanded their entry but plagued the lives of those who dared to imagine a Korea beyond the orbit of the US empire.

Harold Sunoo in Cold War Seattle

Harold Sunoo's life embodied the connections and contradictions of US-Korea relations during the Cold War. Born to a P'yŏngyang family active in the Korean independence movement, he fled Japanese repression for the United States in 1938. Sunoo resumed his anticolonial activities in California, where he pursued higher education. In 1943, he moved to Seattle to teach Korean language and history to American soldiers preparing for deployment in East Asia. At the time, the Army Specialized Training Program at the University of Washington (UW) was the only one in the United States focusing on Korea. After the program shut down, the UW hired Sunoo and his Korean American wife Sonia to continue teaching Korean language and history courses while Sunoo worked toward his doctoral degree.[5]

---

5 Soohee Kim, "The Korean Language Program at the University of Washington: Approaching Its First Seventy Years" (unpublished research paper, University of Washington, Seattle, 2012), 4; Harold Sunoo, *Search for Freedom: A Story of a Korean American* (n.p.: Xlibris, 2004), 99-100.

Sunoo quickly discovered that Japanese colonialism and white supremacy operated on similar logics and registers. When he moved to the Pacific Northwest in 1943, he felt that there was "no room for a Korean in Seattle." He could not find a fellow Korean in the city or a landlord willing to rent him an apartment near the UW. Frustrated, he interrogated the landlords, one of whom told him directly that "the neighbors will complain if I rent this place to other than whites." "That kind of racial discrimination was almost identical as I had experienced in Japan before I came to the US," Sunoo recalled. Johsel Namkung, an accomplished Korean musician who began his studies at the UW in 1948, experienced the same hostility. The only housing that he and his Japanese wife could find was in a Japanese gardener's house in the International District.[6]

Sonia and Harold Hakwon Sunoo taught the first Korean language courses at the University of Washington's Far Eastern Department. Sonia Sunoo later collected and published oral history interviews of Korean Americans in the Pacific Northwest. Courtesy of Harold Sunoo.

------

6 Sunoo, *Search for Freedom*, 106, 304; Johsel Namkung, KAHS Oral History Project, interview with Moon-Ho Jung, Lynnwood, Washington, November 11, 2008.

Sunoo's hope for democracy in Korea contrasted sharply with the US government's policies of military occupation and anticommunism. In Seattle, Sunoo continued his political work by collaborating with a small group of Korean scholars and activists critical of Rhee's right-wing regime in South Korea. Disappointed by the division of Korea and by the US support of South Korea's authoritarian state, Sunoo toured across America with the Civil Rights Congress, a progressive African American organization committed to political freedom during the Cold War. Sunoo also joined the Communist Party of the United States of America at a moment when anticommunist witch hunts drove countless Americans to dissociate themselves from leftist organizations and causes. In 1948, Washington State's anticommunist investigative board, the Canwell Committee, turned its attention to the UW, including Sunoo for his anti-Rhee activities. Sunoo refused to answer court subpoenas on the grounds that the Canwell Committee violated academic and political freedoms.[7]

Sunoo's struggles persisted. The University of Washington dismissed him, despite a recommendation from the Department of Political Science that he be promoted. A combination of racism and anticommunism most likely sealed his fate in the United States. The chair of his Ph.D. committee told him, "I don't believe any Oriental student except the Japanese can . . . obtain a Ph.D. from a first-class university in America." Denied a Ph.D. at the UW, Sunoo eventually obtained his degree in Prague. He returned to teach at various universities in the United States, never stopping his work on behalf of Korean democracy and unification. "I always demonstrated the most dignified, ennobling gesture (I thought) when people asked me if I was a Chinese or Japanese," he stated. "'No,' I would reply proudly, 'I am a Korean.' I was proud of the history of Korea because in Korea's long

---

7 Sunoo, *Search for Freedom;* Bruce Cumings, "Boundary Displacement: Area Studies and International Studies during and after the Cold War," *Bulletin of Concerned Asian Scholars* 29, no. 1 (1997): 17.

history, we had often become the victim of armed aggressions but never the aggressor." For Sunoo, the struggle for Korean liberation informed his understanding of a Korean American identity. "In order to enjoy freedom and justice in America, you must fight for them," he wrote. "We are not guests of this country."[8]

Korean Military Brides and Korean Women's Organizing

US wars fought across the Pacific prompted a new wave of Asian migration to the United States, made up mostly of Asian women who met and married American servicemen stationed overseas. The US government began to repeal laws excluding Asians from the United States, beginning with the Chinese in 1943, South Asians and Filipinos in 1946, and then wives of US military personnel in 1947. Under the McCarran-Walter Act (1952), which finally overturned the 1790 Naturalization Act and institutionalized anticommunism in US immigration law, all Asian women married to US servicemen gained the right to enter the United States. The installation of US military bases in Japan, Okinawa, Korea, and the Philippines (which gained independence from the United States in 1946)—and the establishment of camptowns catering to US military personnel—resulted in a sharp increase in the number of Asian military brides moving to the United States in the 1950s–1970s.[9]

Beginning in the 1950s, American GIs and their Korean brides traveled to the US mainland, especially to the large military bases on the West Coast. Between 1953 and 1960, almost five hundred Korean women arrived in the United States each year as military brides. That number increased to about 1,500 Korean women per year in the 1960s and 2,300 women per year in the 1970s. Between 1950 and

---

8 Sunoo, *Search for Freedom*, 148, 174, 308.

9 Sucheng Chan, *Asian Americans: An Interpretive History* (New York: Twayne, 1991), 140-141; Ji-Yeon Yuh, *Beyond the Shadow of Camptown: Korean Military Brides in America* (New York: New York University Press, 2002), chapter 1. For more on the camptowns in the 1970s and 1980s, see Sandra Pollock Sturdevant and Brenda Stoltzfus, *Let the Good Times Roll: Prostitution and the US Military in Asia* (New York: New Press, 1992), 166-239.

1989, nearly one hundred thousand Korean military brides entered the United States. By the 1970s, nearly six thousand Asian wives of US military personnel lived in the Puget Sound area of Western Washington. According to a survey conducted in 1987, one out of three families stationed at Fort Lewis included foreign-born wives.[10]

The first Korean military bride, Yong Soon Morgan, accompanied her husband, Sergeant John Morgan, to the United States during the Korean War. The newlyweds had met and married in Daegu, South Korea, where Yong Soon had worked as a supervisor of telephone operators. When they stepped off their US Navy transport ship in Seattle on October 18, 1951, the film star Rita Hayworth and a bouquet of red roses greeted the Morgans in what was dubbed "America's traditional family welcome." A parade down Second Avenue followed. The Morgans eventually settled down in Seattle's Central District. On Valentine's Day in 1955, Yong Soon became a naturalized US citizen, just before the couple moved to Japan for Sergeant Morgan's new military assignment. When they returned to Seattle two years later, with their three biracial children in tow, the *Seattle Times* praised the Morgans as an "all-American family."[11]

Other Korean military brides did not receive such accolades. Born in 1951 in South Cholla province, Chun C. Cha had worked in a souvenir store next to a US military base. When her friend married an American military doctor and moved to the United States, the twenty-three-year-old Cha followed her by agreeing to marry a soldier from Syracuse, New York, a man she had never met

10 Chan, *Asian Americans,* 140; Yuh, *Beyond the Shadow of Camptown,* 2; Daniel Booduck Lee, "Marital Adjustment Between Korean Women and American Servicemen," in *Koreans in America: Dreams and Realities,* edited by Hyung-chan Kim and Eun Ho Lee (Seoul: Institute of Korean Studies, 2009), 104.

11 US Information Service, newsreel footage shown in *The Women Outside,* directed by J. T. Takagi and Hye Jung Park (Third World Newsreel, 1995); "1st Korea-War Bride to Land Here Thursday," *Seattle Times,* October 16, 1951; "Some Aliens May Take Short Cut to Citizenship," *Seattle Times,* March 6, 1955; "First Korean War Bride Returns," *Seattle Times,* October 14, 1957.

First Korean War Bride Speechless At City's Greeting

SERGT. JOHN L. MORGAN and bride, YONG SOON
'We didn't expect a big show like this'

The first Korean war bride to arrive in the United States received a welcome this afternoon at Seattle that left her almost speechless.

The bride is Mrs. Yong Soon Morgan, 23, the wife of Sergt. John L. Morgan, 23, of Bremerton.

"She was afraid the American people wouldn't like her," Morgan said.

Reporters on Hand

As newsreel cameramen, magazine and newspaper photographers and reporters pressed around her, the Korean woman smiled happily.

The Morgans arrived on the Navy transport Gen. M. M. Patrick, which docked at 1 o'clock at Pier 39, South.

On the pier to greet the couple were the sergeant's parents, Mr. and Mrs. F. P. Morgan.

As the parents waited for the first sight of their daughter-in-law, they expressed pleasure over their son's choice.

"If she suits him, she suits us; it's just fine," Mrs. Morgan said.

Sergeant Morgan married Lee Yong Soon, daughter of a retired Taegu real-estate man, last February 14, the Korean girl's birthday. Morgan said today they had known each other about a year and a half before they were married. Morgan has been stationed in Korea 42 months.

The Korean bride was overwhelmed by the attention she received when the ship docked. She clung nervously to her tall husband. She is only 5 feet, 1 inch tall.

"We didn't expect a big show,"

like this," Morgan said, after he had been requested by photographers to kiss his young wife for the umpteenth time.

The Korean bride was warmly received by her father-in-law and mother-in-law, when she walked down the gangplank. Her father-in-law kissed her repeatedly before the newsreel cameras.

Also aboard were 382 soldiers, 374 Navy men, 16 marines, 137 military dependents, eight Wacs and 36 civilian employes and dependents. The Patrick was the 36th ship returning Army combat troops from Korea to Seattle.

Al Rochester, city councilman, presented a big bouquet of red roses to the sergeant's wife as a token of friendship of the people of Seattle for the people of Korea.

Nickname is 'Blue'

The Korean bride, whose nickname is "Blue," speaks English fairly well, but she was rendered speechless by the attention she received. She nodded emphatically when asked if she had changed her opinion about how the American people would receive her.

Beverly Michaels, platinum-haired Hollywood starlet, welcomed the sergeant's wife with a kiss. Miss Michaels was at the pier to welcome all the servicemen and dependents who arrived on the Patrick.

Rain let up as the ship docked, and sunshine broke through a few minutes later.

"First Korean War Bride Speechless at City's Greeting," Seattle Daily Times, October 18, 1951. Courtesy of the Seattle Times.

before. After Cha arrived in Syracuse, the couple married and soon moved to Fort Lewis, Washington. Although she eventually found work in seasonal farm labor alongside other military wives, Cha felt isolated and lost in the United States. "I felt as if I were locked up . . . I couldn't even communicate with my husband because of the language barrier," she recalled. "I couldn't socialize with neighbors either. I always felt that I was left alone in a desert." Her marriage eventually fell apart. Dishonorably discharged for refusing to show up for work, Cha's husband began drinking heavily and abusing her. The couple lived in chronic poverty, a situation made worse for Cha when her husband stole her wages. In 1975, she filed for a divorce. Cha was finally able to support herself by working a series of factory and cleaning jobs.[12]

Like Cha, most Korean wives discovered that their new lives rarely met their grand expectations. K. Huntley, a thirty-two-year-old Korean woman who met her military husband at a Korean nightclub, told the *Seattle Times* in 1974, "When I was in Korea, I thought the US was a great country. Now I am disappointed."[13] In addition to cultural and linguistic divides, Korean women experienced an acute sense of dependency in the United States. They relied on their husbands for housing, food, and money. Having met in the racialized and sexualized landscape of Korea—some through commercialized sexual relationships—many of these couples had a difficult time adjusting to their new environs. Women commonly encountered domestic violence, abusive forms of control, and abandonment, against which they had little recourse without language skills, social networks, driver's licenses, and financial resources. When Korean women called the police, for example, their husbands would explain away the complaints to police officers unable or unwilling to provide a hearing for the women. There was

---

12 Chun C. Cha, KAHS Oral History Project, interview with Sun-Hee Yoon, Tacoma, Washington, January 21, 2009.

13 Jan Chrisman, "Fairy Tales Don't Come True: Asian 'War Brides' Face Many Problems," *Seattle Times*, February 17, 1974.

at least one situation at Fort Lewis where a husband denied food to his Korean wife for not obeying his commands.[14]

A survey of Korean military wives in the 1970s attested to their daily struggles in the United States. As part of a broader study of Asian American communities in the Pacific Northwest, Sil Dong Kim, then a graduate student at the University of Washington, conducted a study of Asian-born wives of US military personnel in Seattle, Tacoma, and Fort Lewis. The divorce rate among these couples, she discovered, was nearly 25 percent higher than in either Korea or the United States. Since half of the women had less than six years of formal education before moving to the United States, they generally lacked the resources and opportunities to learn English. Approximately 90 percent of the women Kim surveyed were not fluent in speaking, reading, and writing in English, a predicament that they found extremely frustrating and constraining. One of Kim's interviewees said:

> Even though he beats me up almost every other day, I could not leave him. He brings money in family. Without him, I don't think I could survive. If I have had good brain and English, I wouldn't take this ordeal. I don't have any education. I don't speak English. I don't know how to drive. I have two infants. What can I do? I can't even go back into the street again. I just have to suffer through this until I learn some English and until the kids grow up, I am just stuck to this S.O.B.[15]

Hers was not an exceptional story.

The daily stress of surviving in a strange land consumed many of these women's lives. A state commission on rural Asian

---

14 Lea Armstrong, KAHS Oral History Project, interview with Woonkyong Yeo, Tacoma, Washington, March 16, 2010; Lea Armstrong, KAHS interview with Jessie Kindig, Tacoma, Washington, August 28, 2012; Sil Dong Kim, "Interracially Married Korean Women Immigrants: A Study in Marginality" (Ph.D. diss., University of Washington, 1979).

15 Kim, "Interracially Married Korean Women Immigrants," 102.

American affairs found a similar cycle of isolation and alien-
ation. "The Korean warbrides are isolated and unaccustomed to
the culture, language and lifestyle of white Americans," the commission stated. "It is only after their husbands have abused and
left them that public agencies have often come in contact with
them."[16] Even those living in or near Seattle, where there was a
sizable Korean American population, felt alone. Korean military
wives, however, were by no means mere victims. Recognizing
their common struggles as Korean women, they came together to discuss and address their needs, demands, and aspirations.
Based on their personal histories across the Pacific, these women
would forge their own Korean American identity.

Korean Women's Association
By the 1970s, Korean military wives began to feel a need to establish organizations for themselves. "Most of us here have been
in a same boat all the way," a woman told Sil Dong Kim. "We
had been around the military camp back in Korea and married
one of them to come to the United States. We could talk and understand each other perfectly whereas we don't quite understand
our American husbands or the Seattle Koreans."[17] The number
of Korean military brides in the Tacoma area had grown consid-
erably, alongside Korean businesses and social clubs. In January
1972, Kim Nam Hui convened a group of Korean women in
interracial marriages to start a monthly social club in Tacoma
to share Korean food and personal stories and to help one another with chores. Calling itself the Korean Women's Association (KWA), the group continued for several years primarily as

---

16 Kim, "Interracially Married Korean Women Immigrants"; Reynaldo
Pascua, Jr., *Rural Asian Americans: An Assessment: A Report of the Yakima Valley Asian
American Task Force* (Olympia: Office of the Governor, State of Washington
Commission on Asian American Affairs, 1976), 23.

17 Kim, "Interracially Married Korean Women Immigrants," 108; Yuh, *Beyond
the Shadow of Camptown*, chapter 6.

a place for Korean wives to speak Korean and to create a sense of community.

Over time, the KWA recognized the pressing need for social services. KWA board member Sulja Warnick recalled, "We thought, 'we can do this ourselves!'" In 1976, the KWA applied for city and county funding to expand its scope of work. A grant from Ft. Steilacoom Community College (now Pierce College) launched a series of English classes for Korean military wives. KWA volunteers organized carpools and wake-up calls so that women could attend classes on time. KWA members also organized classes on American-style cooking—a point of persistent contention between husbands and wives—and taught Korean women how to write checks and use American bank accounts. The KWA soon opened these classes to Vietnamese military brides, who began arriving in Tacoma in significant numbers during and after the Vietnam War.

The KWA quickly became a cornerstone of Asian American communities. In 1979, KWA leaders officially designated the group a nonprofit social service organization catering especially to Asian immigrant communities. They organized a variety of programs to meet Korean Americans of all ages, such as a Korean language library and free legal services for older immigrants and a Korean language school and youth programs for children. As word spread, more and more Korean immigrants found their way to the KWA. After discovering a growing elderly population of Koreans in the 1980s, the organization applied to Pierce County for home care service grants to provide free meals and long-term nursing to senior citizens.

The KWA has continued to expand. By the 1990s, a series of federal, state, and county grants funded the association's work and mandated that it provide services to low-income people of all racial backgrounds. Today, the KWA is one of the largest social service agencies in Washington State, serving over 150,000 people from thirty-five different language groups. KWA programs now include: senior home care and meals, domestic violence crisis support, low-income housing, food assistance, and healthcare services. Though it has expanded far beyond Korean military wives, the KWA has retained its grassroots vision and mission. It has "always served the underserved population, the kind of people who could not speak for themselves, voiceless groups, very vulnerable in a way," Warnick states. "We definitely come from our heart and the needs of the community."[18] Through the KWA, legions of Korean women and many others discovered who they were and what they were striving for.

Organizing Korean Adoptees

In addition to Korean women married to American servicemen, US military intervention in Korea resulted in the migration of Korean children to the United States. Beginning in the 1950s, US religious and children's welfare charities turned their atten-

Members of the Korean Women's Association and dignitaries at a ground-breaking ceremony for the KWA Senior City in Federal Way, Washington, September 25, 2008. Courtesy of the Korean Women's Association.

18 Sulja Warnick, KAHS interview with Jessie Kindig (telephone), July 31, 2012; Armstrong, KAHS Oral History Project; Armstrong, KAHS interview with Kindig; "History" and "Services," Korean Women's Association, http://www.kwacares.org/about/history/.

tion to Korean children orphaned during the Korean War. In 1955, Harry and Bertha Holt, an evangelical Christian couple from Eugene, Oregon, received special permission from the US government to travel to Korea and adopt eight Korean orphans fathered by American GIs. The great publicity surrounding their adoption propelled the Holts to found what would become the largest international adoption agency in the United States, Holt International. With an unshakable conviction that American childhood and Christian faith would best serve all children of the world, the Holts initiated a wave of Korean adoptions. It is estimated that between 1958 and 1990, eighty thousand children from Korea were adopted—more than from the rest of the world combined—mostly by white, middle-class American parents. Many ended up in the Pacific Northwest, home to Holt International.[19]

Both the South Korean and American governments adjusted their laws to facilitate the adoption of Korean children. Because of the growing prominence of East Asia in US foreign policy considerations, the US government loosened immigration laws for adoption purposes in the Immigration and Nationality Act of 1961, an exception to the ongoing racial restrictions on immigration from Asia.[20] In the same year, the South Korean government passed a special law encouraging the foreign adoption of Korean children, in part to lessen the need for social services after a devastating war. Particularly for "mixed blood" children, adoption by American parents seemed to offer a better alternative to a life of ostracism in Korea. For the Korean state, it also served as

---

19 Dong Soo Kim, "A Country Divided: Contextualizing Adoption from a Korean Perspective," in *International Korean Adoption: A Fifty-Year History of Policy and Practice*, edited by Kathleen Ja Sook Bergquist et al. (New York: Haworth, 2007), 6-7; and Catherine Ceniza Choy, "Institutionalizing International Adoption: The Historical Origins of Korean Adoption in the United States," in *International Korean Adoption*, 25; Asian Adult Adoptees of Washington State, KAHS interview with Jessie Kindig (telephone), August 6, 2012.

20 Choy, "Institutionalizing International Adoption."

a means to get rid of a subpopulation that defied myths of racial and national homogeneity. What began as a combination of charity, rescue mission, and evangelical work had become, by the 1960s, a lasting and flourishing transpacific institution.[21]

The transnational and, in most cases, transracial adoption of Korean children has had a profound impact on American culture. The incorporation of Korean children into the United States enabled Americans to justify and elide the brutal violence and sexual relations that had characterized the Korean War (and postwar US-Korea relations). Replicating the anticommunist ideology of containment, Americans became, at least in their self-image, the heroic saviors rescuing helpless "orphans," most of whom were not actually orphaned. The institutionalization of Korean adoption reflected and reproduced the uneven and often contradictory interests of the US and Korean governments, private adoption agencies, and Korean and American families. Tens of thousands of adopted children born in Korea and raised in America had to contend with these contradictions every day, as what they came to symbolize— American humanitarianism, progress and development, and multiculturalism—failed to capture the complexities of their lived experiences.[22]

Today, adopted Koreans in the United States comprise a heterogeneous population, spanning several generations and representing varied and contested ideas of racial and national identities. Although the founding image of Korean adoptees from the Korean War—war orphans from a backward country—still lingers in the public imagination, the experiences and positions of Korean adoptees have exceeded and complicated such simplistic

---

21 Kim, "A Country Divided"; Eleana J. Kim, *Adopted Territory: Transnational Korean Adoptees and the Politics of Belonging* (Durham: Duke University Press, 2010), 61-69.

22 Kim, *Adopted Territory*, 48-81. See also Kim Park Nelson, "Korean Looks, American Eyes: Korean American Adoptees, Race, Culture and Nation," (Ph.D. diss., University of Minnesota, 2009).

notions. Over time, Korean adoptees have formed and joined organizations devoted to their particular interests and histories and, in the process, claimed a Korean American identity and community of their own.

The Asian Adult Adoptees of Washington (AAAW) is one such organization. The AAAW originated in December 1996, when a group of adult adoptees met in Seattle to discuss the pressing need for a communal organization to address the enduring sense of isolation that most adoptees feel. Devoted to providing mentoring, educational, and social resources for Asian American and Pacific Islander adoptees, the AAAW serves the needs of persons who often feel alienated from their own families and from Asian American communities. As a member of the AAAW stated, "Being adopted is its own identity." Although Korean adoptees in the United States constitute close to 10 percent of all Korean Americans, they are generally rendered invisible or irrelevant to other Korean Americans' conceptions of the "Korean American community."[23]

The experiences of Korean military brides and adoptees compel us to revisit the haunting legacies of the Korean War and to reflect on what it means to be "Korean," "American," and "Korean American." These are not self-evident categories transcending history but social identities created and re-created by human beings. They are very much rooted in history. It is up to us to figure out their meanings, their relevance to our own lives and to our visions of the future. "There's still so much awareness that needs to be raised around experiences growing up in the US, of families in Korea—those stories are largely unknown and untapped, even by our own community," a member of the AAAW said. The AAAW is engaged in such work, producing formal and informal spaces for adop-

---

23 AAAW, interview with Kindig; AAAW website, http://www.aaawashington.org/
wpress/. For more on Korean adoptees' organizations and shared experiences, see Sunny
Jo, "The Making of KAD Nation," in *Outsiders Within: Writing on Transracial Adoption*, edited
by Jane Jeong Trenka et al. (Cambridge: South End Press, 2006), 285-290.

tees to meet one another, to share stories and resources, and to critique static and exclusionary notions of racial and national identities.[24]

Asian Adult Adoptees of Washington Summer Picnic, 1997. From left to right: Barbara Kim (co-founder), Lisa Mason Hokama, Katie Tupper (co-founder), Cari Kennedy Manvydas (co-founder), and Kennon Konopasek. Courtesy of Katie Tupper.

24 AAAW, interview with Kindig.

CHAPTER THREE

Moving and Building

The number of Koreans in the United States began to sky-rocket in the 1960s. After a century of US immigration laws targeting Asians, Congress passed the Immigration and Nationality Act of 1965, which legally opened the doors to the largest sustained wave of Korean migration to the United States. Beyond legal reforms, the expanding influence of the United States over Korea, perhaps most evident in the form of military deployment and foreign aid, drove millions of Koreans to seek a new life on the other side of the Pacific. In doing so, Korean Americans continued to provide labor to meet the demands of a changing political economy—as blue-collar workers, small business owners, and professionals. But they were more than mere workers. Korean Americans built rich lives outside of work, creating countless political, social, religious, and economic organizations to make the Pacific Northwest their new home.

Post-1965 Migrations

Although lawmakers in the US Congress did not originally intend their immigration bill to accelerate and expand Asian migration to the United States, the Immigration and Nationality Act of 1965 had precisely that ironic effect. Because the law prioritized family reunification—family members of US citizens were exempted from national quotas—many in and outside of Congress imagined that the law would extend historical patterns of immigration favoring northern and western Europeans. "Since the people of . . . Asia have very few relatives here," a sponsor of the bill told his colleagues, "comparatively few could immigrate from those countries because they have no family ties in the US." He would be proven wrong. Between 1965 and 2009, the Asian American population grew from less than 1.2 million to 10.9 million. Koreans made up a sizable percentage of the new migrants. Between 1965 and 2001, 817,390 Koreans entered the United States, increasing the number of Korean Americans more than fifteenfold.[1]

Although migrants and their families made their decisions for very personal reasons, it is imperative that we understand the historical context in which hundreds of thousands of individuals reached the same decision at the same time. The deepening links between South Korea and the United States drove millions of Koreans to dream of moving across the Pacific, at first for further education and then increasingly for professional and personal advancement. But why did they conclude that moving thousands of miles to the United States was their best option? For those seeking further higher education, the choice seemed obvious. Because US missionaries had founded the earliest universities in Korea and the US government took a leading role in establishing Seoul National University after World War II, Korean universities modeled their faculty and curriculum after the US system. As US-trained academics filled the ranks of Korean universities, they formally and informally encouraged their students to seek advanced degrees in the United States. A degree from a US university carried—and continues to carry—prestige in Korea.[2]

---

1   Ronald Takaki, *Strangers from a Different Shore: A History of Asian Americans* (Boston: Little, Brown and Company, 1989), 419; Hyojoung Kim, Hojong Do, and JungJun Park, "The Ascendancy of Second-Generation Korean Americans: Socio-Demographic Profiles of Korean Americans in Washington State," in *Korean American Identities: A Look Forward*, edited by Hyojoung Kim (Seattle: Seattle-Washington State Korean American Association), 9; Mae M. Ngai, *Impossible Subjects: Illegal Aliens and the Making of Modern America* (Princeton: Princeton University Press, 2004), 262.

2   John M. Liu and Lucie Cheng, "Pacific Rim Development and the Duality of Post-1965 Asian Immigration to the United States," in *The New Asian Immigration in Los Angeles and Global Restructuring*, edited by Paul Ong et al. (Philadelphia: Temple University Press, 1994), 83-84.

As access to institutions of higher education widened in Korea, more and more educated professionals decided that migration to the United States would afford better opportunities for employment. With critical support from the US government in the 1960s and 1970s, Park Chung Hee's right-wing dictatorship steered South Korea toward industrial development through the manufacturing of goods for export at low wages. His policies produced contradictions that propelled educated professionals to leave Korea, where they could not find jobs commensurate with their education, for the United States, where immigration reforms and government cuts to higher education created a surging demand for educated professionals. In addition to relatives of US citizens and permanent residents, the 1965 immigration law favored persons with training in science, engineering, and medicine. Amid such national and global conditions and policies, more and more aspiring middle-class Koreans concluded that relocating to the United States would lead to better professional opportunities.[3]

Migration patterns from Korea to the United States shifted dramatically in response. In the late 1960s and early 1970s, the majority of Korean immigrants were professional or skilled technical workers. In 1969, for instance, almost a quarter of those moving from South Korea were professionals with "preferred" immigration status. Although many educated professionals, particularly doctors and nurses, were able to find work in their specialized fields, others found it difficult to meet the credential requirements that states and employers mandated, and increasingly turned to self-employment as small business owners. In 1976, the US Congress passed the Health Professions Educational Assistance Act, which required medical professionals to pass the National Board of Medical Examiners' Examination and to demonstrate competency in written and oral English. The number of Korean doctors and nurses re-

---

3 Paul Ong et al., "The Political Economy of Capitalist Restructuring and the New Asian Immigration," 11-12, 25-26; Paul Ong and Jon M. Liu, "US Immigration Policies and Asian Migration," 53-59; in *The New Asian Immigration*.

David Kim and family arrive in Seattle, 1974. Courtesy of David Kim.

questing US labor certificates declined significantly afterward. Despite this change, the broader shifts in the US political economy continued to drive Koreans to seek new lives across the Pacific. Using the familial provisions of the 1965 law, hundreds of thousands of Koreans moved to the United States to meet the demand for professionals and service workers in the United States.[4]

Seattle and its surrounding areas reflected the rapid rise in the number of Korean Americans. In 1970, the Korean population in Seattle continued to consist primarily of students and their families at the University of Washington. There were 712 Koreans in King County, 477 of whom lived in the city of Se-

---

4 Ong et al., "The Political Economy," 26-27; Ong and Liu, "US Immigration Policies," 60; Kim et al, "Ascendancy," 9; Sucheng Chan, *Asian Americans: An Interpretive History* (New York, Twayne, 1991), 147-148; Ngai, *Impossible Subjects*, 263.

attle. Over the next twenty years, the county's Korean population increased sharply, reaching 12,524 by 1990. At the turn of the twenty-first century, Koreans constituted the sixth largest ethnic group in Washington, numbering 56,438 across the state. Nearly half of the Koreans in Washington resided in King County, while concentrations of Korean residents and businesses emerged and expanded in Federal Way, Tacoma, Shoreline, Edmonds, and Lynnwood.[5] These numerical shifts hardly begin to convey the complexity and heterogeneity of the Korean American population, whose varied histories, experiences, and politics produced a range of community organizations and institutions. In the process of building their families and communities, Korean Americans tackled different issues that gave meanings to their newfound identities in the United States.

Korean Studies at the University of Washington

Originating as a wartime measure in 1943, the Korean language program at the University of Washington (UW) has evolved into one of the largest and most prominent programs for the study of Korean language, culture, and history in the United States. Particularly through the institutionalization of Korean studies, the UW has served as a center for Korean social and political life in Seattle, bringing together faculty, visiting Korean students, and local Korean Americans. The grassroots effort to establish a Korean studies center at the UW in the first decade of the twenty-first century reflected and extended this rich history. Inspired by a collective desire to build lasting institutions to foster the exploration of Korean language and history, Korean Americans in and around Seattle mounted a widespread fundraising drive that compelled the UW to recognize the import of Korean studies, both to the UW and to Korean American communities.

Prior to the great expansion of Korean migration in the 1960s, the UW served as a hub of the Korean American com-

---

5 Census data calculated by Timothy A. Thomas, from the census records of 1970, 1980, 1990, 2000; Kim et al, "Ascendancy."

munity. A small corps of Korean faculty and students had created a "big family" atmosphere, Ick-Whan Lee said, recalling his
arrival as a political science graduate student in 1967. Chang
Hei Lee, the first president of the Seattle-Washington State Korean Association and the founder of the first Korean church in
the region, was then teaching as an instructor at the UW. Lee
and his wife Kannan Kim (Gloria Lee) were known as the "first
couple" among Koreans in Seattle, as they were always helping
to connect Korean international students at the UW with the
surrounding Korean American community. By the late 1960s,
the UW had also become a center for the study of Korean language and history, with a renowned faculty that included Doo
Soo Suh, Fred Lukoff, James Palais, and Bruce Cumings.

For some Korean Americans, Korean studies offered a venue to
explore their own personal histories and identities. Paull Shin, who
would become a prominent senator in the Washington State Legislature, had experienced a series of dislocations not uncommon among
his generation. Living in Seoul as an orphaned teenager, Shin was

*Children bowl at a Korean community picnic, Lincoln Park, 1973. The number of
Korean children increased dramatically after the 1960s. Courtesy of Mansop Hahn.*

adopted by an American GI and brought to the United States after the Korean War. He eventually entered the UW to pursue graduate work in Korean studies. "I had terrible feelings," he remembered of his early days in the United States. "I felt rejected by Korea." Through Korean studies at the UW, Shin was able to regain a personal connection to Korea and to his earlier life.[6]

Despite the program's prominence, the future of Korean studies at the UW remained uncertain. In 1977, with Professor Suh's retirement, there was widespread concern that his faculty position in Korean literature would not be replaced for budgetary reasons. In response, students organized protests and signed petitions, while local Korean American newspapers printed numerous articles and letters on the topic. Park Chung Hee's military dictatorship in South Korea then offered to contribute $60,000 to fund a new faculty position, an offer that could have resolved the impasse. The UW Korean Studies Program faculty, led by James Palais, unanimously voted to refuse the offer and instead expressed their political opposition to Park's regime.

Although the study of Korean language and literature, politics, and history was able to withstand challenges through the 1980s and 1990s, Korean studies faced a major crisis in the early years of the twenty-first century. With the reduction of state funding and the departure of many faculty members, the program's future was shrouded in doubt again. The retirement of James Palais in 2001 acted as a catalyst for Korean Americans in and around Seattle, who mobilized a grassroots campaign to institutionalize Korean studies permanently at the UW. In November 2001, Palais met with State Senator Paull Shin and local community leaders to decide on a course of action. With Ick-Whan Lee, a local businessman who had once studied with Palais, leading the campaign, the drive to save Korean studies at the UW brought Korean

---

6 Daniel Brunell, "Profile: Sen. Paull Shin State Senator, District 21 Senate, Vice President Pro Tem Chair, Higher Education Committee," *Washington Business Magazine* (March/April 2008), 53-54.

Americans together. It was "a beautiful cause," Lee said. "Korean residents here, mostly the first generation, they always think about Korea. We were doing something good for Korea."[7]

The campaign resonated with local Korean Americans. Beginning with a campus rally on March 1, 2002, it attracted throngs of supporters. A community-wide petition drive generated three thousand signatures, while a "ten dollar per head" challenge advertised in the local *Korea Times* brought in $150,000 from more than twelve thousand individual Korean Americans over a three-year period. Local churches, parent-teacher organizations, and young students took up the cause. In addition to lobbying UW and state leaders, the campaign expanded to secure financial and political support from people across the United States and Korea—UW alumni in Korea, South Korean President Kim Dae Jung, and Palais's former students. In 2006, the Center for Korea Studies became a reality. Unlike many philanthropic drives, the campaign for Korean studies rested not on a large donation by a single individual but on a collective effort. "The university and the community had to work together," said Lee. "The university was impressed that the community just rose up to help them. They'd never seen that before."[8]

Religious Institutions

The history of Christianity in Korea, especially its significance to advancing anticolonial nationalism, continued to shape its centrality to Korean American identity in the United States. For many Korean Americans, in the past and in the present, Christian churches have constituted indispensable

---

7 For a detailed history of the Korean programs at the University of Washington, see Soohee Kim, "The Korean Language Program at the University of Washington: Approaching Its First Seventy Years" (unpublished research paper, University of Washington, Seattle, 2012).

8 Ick-Whan Lee, KAHS interview with Chong Eun Ahn and Jessie Kindig, Seattle, Washington, August 2, 2012; Center for Korea Studies, University of Washington, http://jsis.washington.edu/korea/.

centers of communal life, serving simultaneously as refuges from marginalization and discrimination, places of religious faith and congregation, sites of social and political activities, and providers of educational and social services. The rapid

Students rally to save the Korean Studies Program at the University of Washington, 2002. Courtesy Matthew Benuska.

growth of the Korean population in the United States, and the Pacific Northwest in particular, in the 1970s and 1980s led to the founding of many Christian churches in the region and the forging of lasting connections between Christian churches and other Korean American community and political organizations.

The number of Korean churches in and around Seattle has increased dramatically over the last fifty years. Chang Hei Lee led the founding of the first Korean Christian church in Seattle in 1962. Shortly thereafter, Pastor Hye-sung Kim organized church meetings for Korean international students at the UW and helped to found the Korean First Lutheran Church in Tacoma for Korean military brides and their families. With the massive influx of Korean immigrants in the 1970s, the number of Korean churches in the Seattle-Tacoma area grew at a rapid rate: from ten in the 1970s to seventy in the 1980s and 140 in the 1990s. Today, nearly two hundred organized churches and twenty home churches serve the Korean American population in and around Seattle and Tacoma.[9]

The swift growth of Korean Christian institutions in the Pacific Northwest led to the formation of regional church associations in Seattle, Tacoma, British Columbia, and Oregon in the 1980s and in Federal Way in 1996. Regional church and pastors' associations coordinate various activities and functions, serving as unofficial guides to those new to the Pacific Northwest. Many churches hold bilingual worship services every Sunday and offer language classes in English (for new immigrants and elders) and Korean (for children). As they have done historically for the Korean American community, Korean Christian churches in the Pacific Northwest define their role as fostering Christian faith and community life among all Korean Americans and participate in numerous Korean American associations, events, and campaigns.

The Kidok News USA is an example of the vibrancy of Christianity among Korean Americans. Founded by Kim Johng Ho in 1997, the newspaper aimed to spread Christianity through publications and missionary work. Since its first issue, the Kidok News has branched out to publish books, organize pilgrimage trips, promote Christian cultural gatherings and concerts, and organize choir meetings and contests. A former journalist for the *Korea Times* and the *Korea Daily* in the Pacific Northwest, Kim saw his work as fulfilling a social function for the larger Korean American community. The Kidok News and a network of Korean Christian churches in the Pacific Northwest financially support Korean American associations and inspire members to become involved in community celebrations, voter registration drives, and other events. Today, the Kidok News is attempting to

---

9 Hyung-chan Kim, "Korean Christian Churches in the Pacific Northwest: Resources for Korean Ethnic Identity," in *Koreans in America: Dreams and Realities*, edited by Hyung-chan Kim and Eun Ho Lee (Seoul: Institute of Korean Studies, 2009), 177-192; Kim Johng Ho, KAHS interview with Chong Eun Ahn (telephone), September 8, 2012.

organize a federation of all missionary groups based in the state of Washington.[10]

Although the majority of religious Koreans in the United States identify as Christians, there is also a thriving community of Korean Buddhists. During Monk Ilmyŏn's visit to Tacoma in 1983, members of the local Buddhist community asked him to organize a temple in the Pacific Northwest. He subsequently relocated from Korea to Tacoma and helped to found a temple called Seu Mi Sa, meaning "beautiful temple of the west," with support from Buddhists in Korea. The temple was organized to meet the local community's demand and to aid the region's Korean immigrant population. As Monk Ilmyŏn put it, "I wanted Korean immigrants to get together to console each other."

For Chabisim Posal, whose name means "Bodhisattva of the merciful heart," Buddhism offered the most meaningful way to move forward with her life. Finding the congregation at Seu Mi Sa changed her perspective on her personal struggles. She recalled:

> I started coming to the temple when my husband was ill. One of my customers was Buddhist who was attending this temple. One day she came to my shop and asked me to donate [보시]. So I did. Then my husband got sick and she told me to give his name [so that his name is mentioned in prayer]. So I did. I don't think there is anything free in this world. So I went to the temple with some money in an envelope. The hall of the temple was open so I prayed after putting the envelope on the altar. One day I went to the temple but the door of the hall was locked. So I was squatting in front of the window. Then the head monk [주지스님] found me and invited me into his quarter . . . I told the head monk that I have lived my life trying to accept loss [손해보고 살다]. Then the monk told me, "That is Buddhism."[11]

---

10 Kim Johng Ho, KAHS interview with Ahn.

11 Chabisim Posal, KAHS Oral History Project, interview with Sun-Hee Yoon, Tacoma, Washington, May 10, 2009.

Today, Seu Mi Sa serves a congregation of nearly five hundred Buddhists of all racial and ethnic backgrounds. For Monk Ilmyŏn, religious affiliations should not divide communities but bring them together. "Islam, Christianity, and Buddhism all came from the same root," he said. "Allah, God, and Buddha all refer to our mind. We should not try to alienate one another. Instead, we should love each other."[12]

Forging an Asian American Identity

In the late 1960s, a multiracial alliance of students at San Francisco State College and the University of California, Berkeley, went on strike to demand an education relevant to their own experiences and communities. Inspired and influenced by the black freedom movement and estranged and enraged by the Vietnam War, these students helped give birth to ethnic studies, Asian American studies, and an Asian American identity. Rejecting assimilation into the white mainstream, a new cadre of self-identifying Asian Americans forged an alliance with other people of color to generate a radical critique of white supremacy and the US empire. In the late 1960s and 1970s, to claim an Asian American identity was a political act, a move that opened up new ways of seeing and engaging the world, beyond standard American narratives of immigration and assimilation.[13]

Robert Hyung-chan Kim helped to introduce Asian American politics and Asian American studies to the Pacific Northwest. Born and raised in northern Korea, Kim escaped to Seoul and later Busan after the emergence of the communist regime and the Korean War. In 1962, Kim moved to the United States to pursue graduate studies in education. He soon came into contact with the burgeoning African American civil rights movement in

---

12 Buddhist Monk Ilmyŏn, KAHS Oral History Project, interview with Sun-Hee Yoon, Tacoma, Washington, May 10, 2009.

13 See Daryl J. Maeda, *Chains of Babylon: The Rise of Asian America* (Minneapolis: University of Minnesota Press, 2009).

the South. He began participating in lunch-counter "sit ins" with other students at stores that refused to serve people of color. Later, as a first-year faculty member in Auburn, Alabama, he taught classes on discrimination, racism, and integration. Kim moved west to take up a new faculty position teaching Asian American studies at Western Washington University (WWU) in Bellingham.

At the time, Asian American studies was an emergent field, more of a collective idea and vision than an established course of study. Kim recalled:

> There's really . . . no[t] any kind of concerted effort on the part of scholars to produce books dealing with Asian American community as far as I know. . . . So I began to do research, then I decided, "OK, first of all, I will do some research that would create basis for Asian American studies." That's how I decided to write the *Dictionary of Asian American History*. I thought that that was the fundamental base, because that was one way to define what Asian American history was. . . . So I guess, in some ways, my attempt was to define the discipline, or the interdisciplinary field of Asian American studies.

Beyond writing some of the earliest scholarly works in the field, Kim helped to institutionalize Asian American studies. After an initial meeting at the University of Washington in 1979, Kim and a handful of professors became the founding members of the Association for Asian American Studies, now the most prominent organization in the field.

Putting into practice the vision that had motivated student and community activists in the 1960s, Kim taught his students to identify with a larger community and history. As part of his course on "Asian American Community" in the early 1970s, he took small groups of undergraduates to Seattle and Vancouver to interview elderly Asian American residents. On many occasions, Kim and his students became involved in local political campaigns.

In Seattle, they joined the protests against the construction of the Kingdome sports stadium next to the International District, planting themselves on the front lines.[14] Kim remembered:

> We, students and I sat in front of bulldozers; bulldozers came and rattled the buildings, and we sat there and protested. . . . There were a lot of old-timers who didn't have any place to go to, because this was before the senior housing was made available. That's what we did. Then I would take students to Vancouver. Vancouver City was at the same thing, . . . what they did was to clean up urban ghetto which included all the Chinese tenements. So we went there and interviewed, and also protested and signed petitions. That's how I taught Asian American Community.

The struggle to save Seattle's International District in the early 1970s placed the needs of the International District's residents ahead of those of tourists, spawning a movement that was explicitly pan-Asian. Although Kim was perhaps the only Korean involved in the movement early on, he believes its collective ethos affords lessons for today's Korean Americans. Korean American youth should become active "participants in democracy," he advised. "They should know who they are and where they came from. At least, they should know where their parents came from and then where they came from, so that they will have some sense of continuity."[15]

---

14 Trevor Griffey, "Seattle's Asian American Movement," special section of the Seattle Civil Rights and Labor History Project http://depts.washington.edu/civilr/aa_intro.htm.

15 Robert Hyung-chan Kim, KAHS Oral History Project, interviews with Moon-Ho Jung and Woonkyung Yeo, Mukilteo, Washington, December 17, 2009 and January 22, 2010.

Labor and Legal Struggles as Korean Americans

If the vast majority of Korean Americans in the Pacific Northwest were not active participants in the Asian American movement, they nonetheless inherited its causes and aspirations. In spite of (or perhaps because of) their growing numbers, Korean Americans in Seattle recognized the need to combat anti-Asian racism by organizing themselves. By the early 1970s, Korean Americans had become a visible presence in Seattle's shipyards, employed mostly as blue-collar workers. Korean American welders came together to form a loose organization to address their needs in 1973 and, with the expansion of their ranks, formalized themselves as the Korean Technicians' Association (KTA), which included painters, pipefitters, and sheet metal workers. In southwest Seattle, KTA members ran a welding school with classes in Korean to train recent immigrants for work in the shipyards.

Tensions reached a boiling point in the late 1970s, by which time about seven hundred Korean Americans worked on Seattle's waterfront. Many white workers resented the hiring of Korean Americans, while employers treated Korean American workers unfairly. In 1979, things turned ugly when anti-Korean graffiti began appearing on the restroom walls of Harbor Island's shipyard facilities. In a KTA meeting called to address the issue, a former employee of the Lockheed and Todd Shipyards reported that anti-immigrant and anti-Asian slogans were posted in many of the company's workshops. Other Korean American workers voiced their protests over unfair firings, penalties, and abuses inflicted by the management. In 1980, in a meeting with Dolores Sibonga, a Filipina American member of the city council, KTA members petitioned for a more comprehensive English "survival language program" to learn "how to deal with unfair treatment and how to address problems through formal channels." Legal action against their employers proved far too difficult, but the KTA recognized the need for Korean American workers to band together.[16]

Both individually and collectively, many Korean Americans drew the same conclusion. After moving from Korea to New Jersey when he was twelve years old, Sam Chung witnessed the daily struggles Korean immigrants confronted, including those of his parents who ran a grocery store in Jersey City. Hoping to make a difference, he decided to pursue a law degree. Chung said:

> I saw a lot of people with problems that they cannot solve and it overwhelmed them because of language and cultural barriers . . . just getting a statement from public utility or just not being able to decipher and comprehend things that are happening to them. And the feeling of powerlessness, that you're not capable of resolving those issues on your own, that made people very . . . weak. Observing that and growing up with those types of things around me, I thought that would be a good job to get into.

In the early 1990s, when an endless series of media reports on the supposed Korean-black conflict put the spotlight on Korean Americans across the United States, Chung recognized an acute need for Korean Americans to organize and represent themselves. In 1991, he helped to found a Washington chapter of the Korean American Bar Association to provide legal clinics and to establish a network of Korean American lawyers and law students. Through his work, the Korean American community in and around Seattle gained access to free legal counseling from Korean American attorneys, helping to bridge generational and professional divides.[17]

---

16 Kun Hong Park, "'Go Back to Your Country!': Korean Workers Were Resented at Seattle Shipyards," *Occasional Papers of the Korean American Historical Society* 3 (1997): 85-94.

17 Sam Chung, KAHS Oral History Project, interview with Sun-Hee Yoon, Seattle, Washington, March 20, 2009.

Mel Kang was one of the Korean American attorneys who volunteered at the free legal clinics. Back in the 1960s and 1970s, Kang had worked with Mexican and Filipino American farmworkers in the movement to win labor and union rights in California. It was there that he realized how the law could be used to advance social justice. Kang recalled:

> I remember when I was organizing and when I was picketing [with the farmworkers] in LA, we had a letter from a lawyer that said we had the right to picket on private property. And at that time, the state of the law was you did have that right in shopping centers. And so I was quite amazed because when the cops came to kick us off the property, we just showed him that letter and he read it and goes "oh OK," and he let us picket. And I thought, man, that is amazing. So I remembered that, when I decided to take labor law and go to law school.

When he moved to Seattle in the early 1980s, Kang worked for the National Labor Relations Board investigating unfair labor practices.

In addition to volunteering at legal clinics, Kang is also one of several Korean Americans active in the Seattle chapter of the Asian Pacific American Labor Alliance (APALA), a national organization founded in 1992 to address issues related to Asian American and Pacific Islander workers. Kang's work attests to the multiplicity and fluidity of social and political identities. Korean, Korean American, Asian American, worker—these are not fixed states of being but collective identities through which we can discover, define, and at times realize our visions for a better world.[18] As Sam Chung noted, "Every once in a while, you see

---

18 Mel Kang, KAHS Oral History Project, interview with Sun-Hee Yoon and Hwasook Nam, Seattle, Washington, March 24, 2009; Mel Kang, KAHS Oral History Project, interview with Sun-Hee Yoon, Moon-Ho Jung, and Hwasook Nam, Seattle, Washington, May 22, 2009.

From left to right: Washington State Supreme Court Justices Charles Johnson, Steven Gonzalez, and Mary Yu with Mel Kang and Sam Chung at the Korean American Bar Association's Twentieth Anniversary Gala. Courtesy of Matthew Benuska.

justice happening to these people who always had thought that law was outside their realm of possibility and they relish it and think it's the greatest thing in the world. It doesn't happen every day, but every once in a while it does happen and kind of makes the things go round."[19]

Struggles for Democracy Across Borders

For generations, Korean Americans have maintained close ties to their ancestral homeland. Like their forebears, post-1965 immigrants have kept abreast of political developments in Korea through community newspapers, letters with loved ones in Korea, and conversations at church. After mass protests deposed Syngman Rhee, Park Chung Hee engineered a military coup in 1961 and began to rule South Korea with an iron fist. Chun Doo Hwan's succession to the presidency after Park's assassination in 1979 extended the authoritarian trajectory of South Korean politics, in which bloody state repression attempted to extinguish fierce and persistent cries for social justice. Struggles for democ-

---

19 Sam Chung, KAHS interview.

racy in South Korea in the 1970s and 1980s came to define not only Korean politics but also a Korean American identity among a generation of political activists in the United States.[20]

Sue Sohng's life was very much shaped by the movement to democratize Korea. Her family had been involved in the struggle for independence from Japanese colonial rule and opposed Syngman Rhee's regime. Sohng began to carry on her family's political tradition in college. She became a political organizer at Yonsei University, but a wave of political

Korean American Bar Association President Michelle Chen speaks with volunteer attorneys and interpreters at the Foreclosure Prevention Clinic, organized by KABA and the Northwest Justice Project, 2011. Courtesy of Matthew Benuska.

repression by Park's regime forced her to move to the United States to escape arrest. While working low-wage jobs and earning graduate degrees in Detroit, Michigan, Sohng and her husband continued to fight for political change in Korea. They found kindred spirits in the United States. With a nationwide network of Korean American activists, they eventually helped organize a pro-democracy newspaper, *Dongnopshinmun*, published in Philadelphia and distributed to Korean communities across the United States and Europe. Women,

---

20 Bong-youn Choy, *Koreans in America* (Chicago: Nelson-Hall, 1979), 213-215.

Sohng recalled, were central to the movement. "Even in this meager anti-military democratic movement, it was all women power," she said. "And many others in the '70s who devoted themselves to this anti-military activism in America, many of their wives were nurses. When you look at every single one of those names, women held the family together." It was these women's work and wages that made *Dongnopshinmun* possible.

All of her political work to democratize Korea, Sohng discovered, had transformed her outlook, her identity. Sohng and her husband had always intended to return to Korea, a plan they were able to fulfill once South Korea made the transition to democratic elections in 1988. Although their political activities had tied them intimately to Korea, they were surprised to discover they felt out of place there. "We were away for fifteen years, when the most intense period of political transformation was happening," she said. "I kind of felt that there wasn't a place for us. We weren't part of that struggle; we weren't part of witnessing that historical transformation. . . . That was utterly awakening . . . because all these years, our identity had been Korean." In 1994, Sohng returned to the United States to take up a faculty position at the University of Washington, where she works closely with Seattle's Asian American and Pacific Islander organizations. "This is the community I have to root myself in," she said.[21]

Jean Kim likewise moved to the United States for political reasons. She and her husband Kim Donggeon left Korea in 1971 to escape political repression and financial hardship. They had supported Kim Dae Jung, the opposition leader in Korea, and continued their work toward Korean democracy in St. Louis, Missouri. In 1979, they moved to Lynnwood, Washington, where Jean Kim began a career in social work and her husband opened an Asian grocery store. They continued to receive news of events in Korea, most notably Park's assassination followed

---

21 Sue Sohng (Sung Sil Lee), KAHS Oral History Project, interview with Moon-Ho Jung, Seattle, Washington, May 4, 2009.

by Chun's military coup. Chun proceeded to declare martial law and to outlaw all political protests and activities. When students in Gwangju, the capital of South Cholla province in southwest Korea, organized protests against Chun's orders, military paratroopers cracked down hard. The citizens of Gwangju rose up in response, briefly driving local police and national troops out of their city. Chun ordered the troops back in and unleashed a bloody wave of violence that would haunt Gwangju for decades. Hundreds of civilians, many of them young students, were killed.

The Gwangju Massacre inspired Kim and her husband to organize against Chun's regime. "We saw picture of young kids that were killed in Gwangju: they were all tied with their hands behind their back, and stabbed to death," she recalled. "We could not tolerate that. . . . We formed the Washington State Korean Human Rights Council, and we were part of National Human Rights Peace and Democracy Movement in Korea." When Chun subsequently visited Seattle as South Korea's president, the Kims helped to organize a protest outside the Westin Hotel, where he was staying, and successfully blocked the front door to the building. "He had to get in and out through garbage door," Kim remembered. "And he had all kinds of plan to visit some churches, do boating on the water, and all kinds. He cancelled everything, stayed in hotel, and left. So we made a coffin and carried that as we demonstrated. That was very sensational."

The protests enabled the Kims to expand their political community, but simultaneously stirred fears and divisions among Korean Americans. They received support from local Seattle news stations and newspaper reporters, university faculty and students, and other human rights organizations working against apartheid in South Africa and Ferdinand Marcos's dictatorship in the Philippines. The media attention helped to protect the Kims from Chun's *ggangpae* (gangsters), who had arrived in Seattle in advance of his visit to intimidate local activists and deter them from proceeding with their protests. Indeed, many Korean students and Korean Americans in Seattle felt that they could not take the risk, fearing that the South Korean government would retaliate against them or their families in Korea. Conservative Korean Americans, on the other hand, criticized the Kims for their politics. Calling the Kims "communists"—a charge that Jean Kim found especially reprehensible, given that she had fled North Korea during the Korean War and lost many family members there—they boycotted Kim Donggeon's grocery store, which was forced to go out of business. The couple was even asked to leave a Sunday church service. These experiences deepened Jean Kim's re-

A protester, playing a soe *and wearing* minbok, *steps on an effigy of South Korean President Chun Doo Hwan in Seattle, April 19, 1986. Courtesy of Dean Wong.*

solve to work for social justice. She became a Christian pastor working with homeless women and college students in the Seattle area.[22]

It is tempting to narrate Korean American history—and American history in general—as a story of immigration and assimilation, as if "Koreanness" and "Americanness" could be measured definitively against each other. From the first generation to the second generation and so forth, Koreans have learned

---

22 Jean Kim, KAHS Oral History Project, interview with Woonkyung Yeo, May 16, 2010; Jean Kim, KAHS Oral History Project, interview with Moon-Ho Jung, Woonkyung Yeo, and Chong Eun Ahn, June 1, 2010.

to become more "American," or so the mythical tale of the American Dream tells us. The portraits included in this chapter suggest a different story, a story of struggle that transcends generations and national borders. What does it mean to be Korean American? There is no single answer, for it is in the process of exploring and debating our past and our future that we come to define our collective identities. It is an endless process. Some Korean Americans—like those who labeled the Kims "communists" and kicked them out of their church—might find such notions insensible. These Korean Americans think they know who they are and what they stand for. Such static and reactionary ideas will lead Korean American communities into oblivion. By recognizing individuals and institutions who may not represent typical Korean Americans, we can perhaps begin the process of building new histories, identities, and communities.

Brother-in-law, a bank School Teach...

CHAPTER FOUR

Contemporary Profiles

The number of Korean Americans has continued to increase dramatically. By 2010, Koreans constituted the fourth largest Asian ethnic group in Washington State—after the Chinese, Filipinos, and Vietnamese—and the sixth largest ethnic group in the state overall. New Korean immigrants continue to move to the Pacific Northwest and Washington in particular, especially along the Puget Sound's urban corridor from Everett to Olympia. Recent immigrants make up the vast majority (about two-thirds) of the Korean American population, both in the United States and in Washington. The number of Korean immigrants relocating across the Pacific was higher in the first decade of the twenty-first century than it was in the 1980s, the previous peak.[1]

Korean Americans established numerous organizations since the 1990s to address the needs of the growing Korean American population. From small business associations to political advocacy and voter registration drives, Korean American organizations strive to meet the daily political, economic, and social needs of their constituencies. Building on the work of many of the individuals and institutions discussed in the previous two chapters, some of these organizations critically explore and challenge

---

1 Unless noted otherwise, all statistics in this chapter are calculated by demographer Timothy A. Thomas of the University of Washington, and based on the 2010 US census and the American Community Survey, a detailed yearly demographic survey run by the US Census Bureau.

prevailing notions of Korean American identity and attempt to forge alliances with other groups to address issues of social justice. What follows are snapshots of today's Korean Americans in and around Seattle, a complex and heterogeneous population that is continuously defining and refining what it means to identify as Korean American and to build a lasting community.

Korean Americans in US Census Data, 2010

All people identifying as Korean in the United States—Koreans, Korean Americans, and Korean as part of a multiracial identity (hereafter referred to collectively as "Koreans")—numbered 1,706,822 in 2010, a 38.9 percent increase since 2000. Of these, 111,161 Koreans live in the Pacific Northwest, with the highest concentration in Washington. There are 6,542 Koreans in Alaska, 2,806 in Idaho, 1,369 in Montana, 20,395 in Oregon, and 80,049 in Washington. Washington's Korean population increased by 23,611 residents between 2000 and 2010 and now makes up nearly 13 percent of the state's Asian population. The majority of Koreans in Washington (55 percent) are female.[2]

In Washington, most Koreans live in the western corridor encompassing Everett, Seattle, Federal Way, Tacoma, and Olympia. There are also concentrations of Koreans in Clark County, next to Portland, Oregon, and around Spokane in Eastern Washington (see figure 1). In Western Washington, Seattle is home to the greatest number of Koreans (8,682), followed by Federal Way (5,303), Bellevue (4,912), Tacoma (3,880), and Lakewood (2,412). Of these municipalities, Tacoma, Seattle, and Lakewood report the highest percentage of multiracial Koreans, reflecting

---

2 In 2000, the US Census Bureau began allowing respondents to mark multiple racial identities. The figures here count anyone claiming Korean racial identity, either alone or in combination with other racial and ethnic identities. Please note that the US census counts "Filipino" as a race, not a subgroup of Asian ethnicity. As a result, Filipina/os are not counted as part of the overall "Asian" population of the United States, unless a census respondent claims a dual Asian/Filipino racial identity.

a history of military marriages and a higher rate of interracial marriages among second- and third-generation Korean Americans. In contrast, greater percentages of Koreans claiming only Korean as their racial identity reside in Federal Way and Bellevue, most likely indicating higher numbers of recent immigrants.

Despite the relatively high concentration of Koreans in and around Seattle, US census records suggest that Koreans are increasingly moving to other parts of Western Washington. Since the 1970s, the growth of the Korean population has not kept pace with the overall population growth in King County. More and more recent immigrants from Korea are moving to Pierce, Snohomish, and Thurston counties, perhaps because of the lower costs of living (see figure 2). Seattle and King County, however, remain the main hub of Asian American communities in the Pacific Northwest. Of all the municipalities in the United States, Seattle reports the eleventh highest concentration of Asians. Despite the recent dispersion to new areas, Korean immigrants continue to gravitate to regions in the Pacific Northwest where other Korean Americans and Asian Americans reside (see figure 3).

Korean-owned businesses at Eunia Plaza, Highway 99, Lynnwood, Washington. Courtesy of Matthew Benuska.

Because most Koreans in Washington—or their parents— moved to the United States after 1965, the population is relatively young. One out of every four Koreans in Washington is between the ages of fifteen and twenty-nine. Born between 1981 and 1995, most of the Korean Americans in this age group are probably children of Korean immigrants who moved to the

United States in the late 1970s and 1980s. Almost half (46.3 percent) of all Koreans in Washington are under the age of thirty. The percentages of Koreans in their thirties (15 percent), forties (13 percent), and fifties and early sixties (17 percent) represent the varied and related histories of military brides, Korean adoptees, and children and parents of recent immigrants.

Data on places of birth also underscore the rapid increase in Korean immigration since 1965. In 2010, nearly 65 percent of the Korean population in the United States reported that they were born outside the United States, typically in Korea. That percentage was slightly lower in Washington State, where about 60 percent identified Korea as their country of birth and 38 percent claimed they were born in the United States. Small numbers of Koreans were born in other locations—mostly other

Figure 1

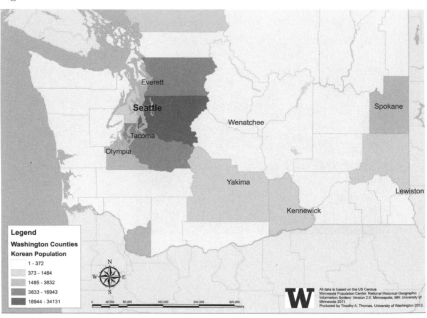

Figure 2

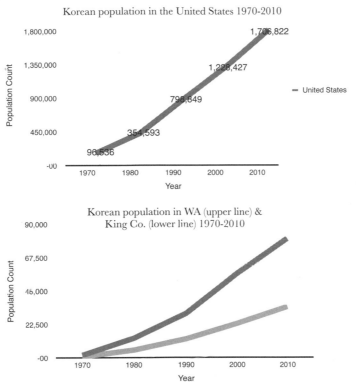

Korean population in the United States 1970-2010

Korean population in WA (upper line) &
King Co. (lower line) 1970-2010

Asian countries or US territories and military bases overseas—
before they moved to the United States. Many of those born
outside the United States arrived during the peaks of Korean
immigration in the 1980s (254,873 to the United States, 13,117
to Washington) and the first decade of the twenty-first century
(317,824 to the United States, 13,765 to Washington). Most foreign-born Korean Americans in the United States have become
naturalized citizens (52 percent); a smaller but significant number (4 percent) already had US citizenship before entering the
country. Both figures are a bit higher in Washington State (see
figure 4).

Using and passing on the Korean language remains central to many Korean Americans' sense of a collective identity. Thirty percent of Koreans in the United States list English as their only language, while 70 percent report an Asian/Pacific Islander language (most likely Korean) as their primary language. About 40 percent of Koreans in

Figure 3

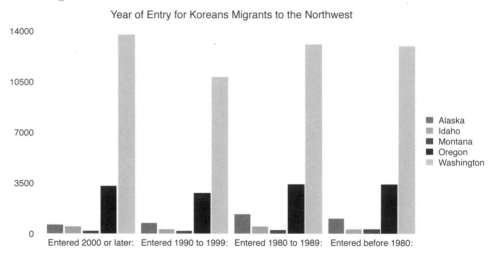

Year of Entry for Koreans Migrants to the Northwest

the United States can communicate in more than one language. Figures for Washington State are about the same. For more than a century, Koreans in the United States have organized classes and schools to teach younger generations the Korean language. Most schools had been small, run by individual churches, until Korean Americans in and around Seattle saw the need to consolidate them to serve the expanding population. With financial support from the South Korean government and the coordinated efforts of fourteen local Korean churches, Korean American community leaders established United Korean Schools in Seattle in 1995 and in Bellevue in 1997.[3] Together the two schools serve 550 students every weekend.

Korean Americans work in a variety of fields and occupations. The vast majority of Koreans in Washington are wage and salary workers in the private sector, as opposed to being self-employed or working in the public (government) sector. The largest number of Koreans are employed in the fields of social assistance, health care, and education (18 percent), followed by: retail trade (15 percent); arts, recreation, food services, and accommodation (15 percent); and professional, scientific, management, and administrative services (13 percent). These numbers point to a class bifurcation among Korean Americans, who are divided roughly equally between professional white-collar occupations and service-based retail jobs. More women than men are employed in service, sales, and office occupations, while men outnumber women slightly in business, science, management, and the arts (see figure 5).

On the surface, Koreans appear to be financially successful, but statistics can obscure a more complex picture. Korean families in Washington reported a median family income ($60,648 per year) higher than the state's overall median family income ($56,850). Particularly in light of the "model minority" stereotype, a racial label projected onto Asian Americans since the 1960s, such numbers can be very misleading. Asian Americans tend to have greater numbers of family members contributing to the household income. And across the United States, Asian Americans, including Korean Americans, live in areas where the cost of living is very high.[4] Sixty thousand dollars in Seattle is not

---

3 Ick-Whan Lee, KAHS interview with Chong Eun Ahn and Jessie Kindig, Seattle, Washington, August 2, 2012; Soohee Kim, "The Korean Language Program at the University of Washington: Approaching Its First Seventy Years" (unpublished research paper, University of Washington, Seattle, 2012).

4 Sucheng Chan, *Asian Americans: An Interpretive History* (New York: Twayne, 1991), 167-168.

Figure 4 (Three-Year Estimates, 2010)

Koreans entering the U.S.: 1,107,289

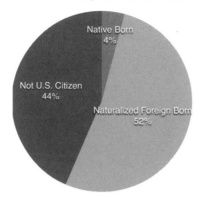

Koreans entering Idaho: 1,734

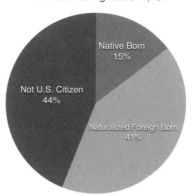

Koreans entering Alaska: 3871

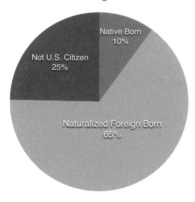

Koreans entering Montana: 988

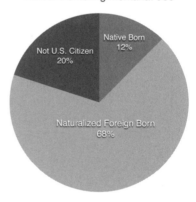

Koreans entering Oregon: 13,036

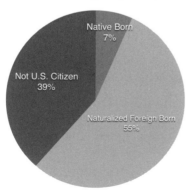

Koreans entering Washington: 50,698

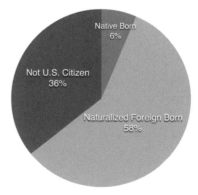

Dr. Soohee Kim, who teaches at the University of Washington, leads a class of middle and high school students at the United Bellevue Seattle Korean School (Seattle campus), September 20, 2014. Courtesy of Julie Kang.

the same as $60,000 in Pullman. Cumulative statistics on income can also mask great disparities among Korean Americans, such as a significant gender gap. The median individual income was $49,124 for Korean men and $37,241 for Korean women.

Rocky Kim and Korean American Small Businesses

Like many Koreans, Yongsu "Rocky" Kim moved from South Korea to Los Angeles in 1972, with plans to finish a degree in electrical engineering, but he turned to small business instead. When he relocated to Washington State in 1981, he opened a grocery store and deli in Lynnwood and then moved on to own and operate a gas station and minimart in West Seattle. Many of his contemporaries followed the same path and recognized the need for an organization to represent their interests. In 1985, they founded the Korean American Grocers Association of Washington (KAGRO), with Kim as president. As lawyer Mel Kang recalled, Kim became involved in KAGRO "because he wanted to be able to deal with vendors who were not treating the grocers fairly, who were extracting deals out of them that

Figure 5 (2010)

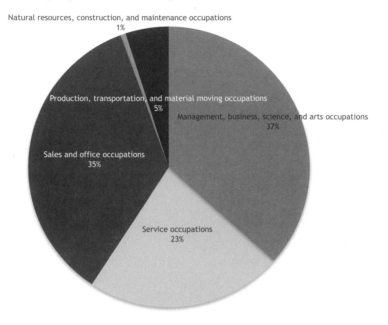

Female civilian employed population 16 years and over

Natural resources, construction, and maintenance occupations
1%

Production, transportation, and material moving occupations
5%

Management, business, science, and arts occupations
37%

Sales and office occupations
35%

Service occupations
23%

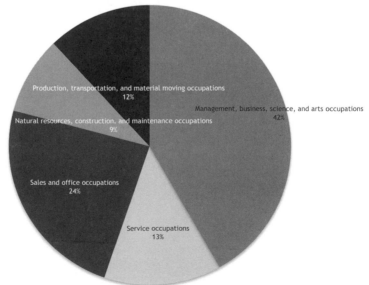

Male civilian employed population 16 years and over

Production, transportation, and material moving occupations
12%

Management, business, science, and arts occupations
42%

Natural resources, construction, and maintenance occupations
9%

Sales and office occupations
24%

Service occupations
13%

they were [not] getting out of other people and stuff like that." KAGRO played an instrumental role in helping small business owners become familiar with legal and regulatory matters, form a social and political network with one another, and make their industry more equitable.[5]

Over the next fifteen years, Kim served as an important spokesperson for the Korean American community. He continued to represent the interests of Korean small business owners by working as a liaison to city agencies and regulatory boards and making sure regulatory materials were available in Korean. Kim also helped to build bridges between Korean immigrants and mainstream non-Korean political candidates. He served on the boards of the Korean American Professionals Society and the Asian Counseling and Referral Service. After Kim was tragically murdered at his West Seattle gas station on October 30, 2000, friends remembered him as the heart and soul of Western Washington's Korean American community. At the funeral, Governor Gary Locke said that Kim "gave a voice to others who might not have been heard. He made life better (for his community and) beyond the Korean community."[6]

Kim's murder illustrates the great risks that many Korean American small business owners confront every day. Their struggles had become evident in the late 1980s and early 1990s, when a barrage of news reports on the "Korean-black conflict" turned the public's attention to Korean grocery store owners, from New York City to Los Angeles. On April 29, 1992, (referred to as Sa-I-Gu by Korean Americans), the acquittal of four white police officers involved in the beating of black driver Rodney King un-

---

5 Mel Kang, KAHS Oral History Project, interview with Sun-Hee Yoon and Hwasook Nam, Seattle, Washington, March 24, 2009; Mel Kang, KAHS Oral History Project, interview with Sun-Hee Yoon, Moon-Ho Jung, and Hwasook Nam, Seattle, Washington, May 22, 2009; Keiko Morris, "Local Korean Leader Shot Dead," *Seattle Times*, October 31, 2000.

6 Morris, "Local Korean Leader"; Assunta Ng, "Some 1,000 gather to remember Rocky Kim," *Korea Times*, January 8, 2001.

leashed three days of rage and violence in Los Angeles, directed most prominently at Korean-owned mom-and-pop stores. Korean Americans lost 2,300 businesses, which accounted for more than half of the one billion dollars of property that went up in flames in the spring of 1992. Seven years later, only a third had reopened for business.[7]

Based on Kim's vision—a vision he shared with so many Korean American small business owners—KAGRO aspires to give voice to those who had no voice in Los Angeles in 1992. Over the years, KAGRO has grown to encompass six chapters with 850 individual members across Washington State. Today, according to the organization, there are roughly 950 Korean American retailers across Washington. Together they generate two billion dollars in revenue every year and employ 1,500 non-Koreans. The majority of **KAGRO** members are immigrants whose as-

Rocky Kim (standing far left) joins a ceremony where Governor Gary Locke (seated) signs a bill designating May as Asian Pacific American Heritage Month. State Senator Paull Shin (standing immediately next to Governor Locke) was the prime sponsor of the bill in 2000. Courtesy of Matthew Benuska.

---

7 Ronald Takaki, *Strangers from a Different Shore: A History of Asian Americans* (Boston: Little, Brown and Company, 1989), 440-444; Helen Zia, *Asian American Dreams: The Emergence of an American People* (New York: Farrar, Straus and Giroux, 2000), chapter 7.

pirations for advanced degrees and professional careers shifted to practicalities of running small businesses.[8] Korean American small business owners represent Korean Americans to the larger society in many ways. In neighborhood gas stations and grocery stores, teriyaki restaurants, dry cleaners, and other small businesses across Washington, they put in an extraordinary amount of time and energy every single day to make ends meet. Their labor shapes so many people's daily lives, in remarkable ways that often escape notice.

Polycultural Korean Americans

"What are you?" That is a question that haunts multiracial Korean Americans and, really, anyone who does not fit readily into predominant notions of race. Sometimes it is an innocent question. Most times it is not. It often raises questions of authenticity, since responses of "half Korean" or "quarter Korean" seemingly can never quite equal a more unequivocal "Korean." These sentiments can be expressed in the most unexpected moments and contexts, as when a former board member of the Korean American Historical Society derisively called multiracial Korean Americans "nothing but mutts." Presumably, he saw himself as a paragon of Koreanness, the undisputed Korean of the world. (There is a reason why he is a former board member.) We must reject such ideas of identity and authenticity that would have us believe that Koreanness can be measured somehow—biologically, culturally—as if there are essential qualities to being a Korean.

Every single human being in the modern world is, as historian Robin D. G. Kelley puts it, "polycultural." It is not to suggest that everyone looks or acts the same; all peoples are products of different cultures that are constantly in flux. There is no single Korean culture that has remained unchanged for the past five millennia, just as there is no single, unchanging American culture. Culture by definition has been and

8 Korean American Grocers' Association, http://kagrowa.org/about_us_eng. html.

always will be fluid and hybridized. The notion of a Korean identity emerged in particular contexts over the last century, for example, amid struggles against Japanese colonialism. "Mixed race" Korean Americans may embody the history of intimate relations between Korea and the United States, but so do the rest of us. All Korean Americans are here as a result of those relations. No one can be racially pure, since race is a modern concept rooted in false notions of biological differences. We are all polycultural, impure human beings. Those impurities are perhaps more visible on some of our faces and in some of our skin colors, but this heterogeneity should invite us not to claim a kind of purity or authenticity but rather to recognize and appreciate impurities all around and within us.[9]

The US census is beginning to acknowledge the complexity of racial categories. Since 2000 it has allowed people to identify themselves as belonging to more than one racial category, but that is not enough. We should also recognize the enduring power of race. It is more than a box (or boxes) we check off every ten years. We are definitely not all viewed or treated alike. Of all

	Number of Multiracial Koreans	Percentage of Multiracial Koreans among Entire Korean Population
Washington	17,675	22%
Alaska	1,858	28%
Idaho	1,136	41%
Montana	532	39%
Oregon	5,183	25%

9 Robin D. G. Kelley, "Polycultural Me," *Utne Reader* (September-October 1999).

self-identified Koreans in Washington State, 17,675 list at least one other racial or ethnic identity (22 percent of the total Korean population). Percentages of multiracial Koreans are higher in other states in the Pacific Northwest.

Multiracial Koreans also list white, black, American Indian or Alaska Native, Chinese, Asian Indian, Filipino, Japanese, Vietnamese, Native Hawaiian, Chamorro, Samoan, Hispanic, or another ethno-racial category. We are the world, in a sense. Although we should take pride in all of our ancestral backgrounds, we cannot conflate or equate them all. To identify as Native Hawaiian (Kanaka Maoli), Alaska Native, or American Indian, for example, often demands reckoning with a history of ongoing colonialism, just as claiming a black identity tends to lead others to make racial assumptions very different from those people make of Koreans.[10]

Eliaichi Kimaro (second from right) and her family. Kimaro's award-winning documentary film, A Lot Like You *(2012), explores the intricacies of multiracial identity, family, and culture. Photograph by Laura van Dernoot Lipsky.*

---

10 The US census began allowing respondents to mark multiple races/ethnicities in 2000. In 1950, the census moved from a fill-in-the-blank racial category to a check mark system. "Korean" was added as an option in 1970. As of today, "Korean" is a "detailed group" within the "Asian" race, as are "Japanese," "Chinese," and other ethnic groups.

As the Korean Women's Association did in the 1970s, community organizations have emerged to address the needs of multiracial Korean American families. By 2000, marriages between Korean women and non-Korean men were different from the military marriages of the 1950s–1980s in some ways. Many of the Korean women who are part of these unions today are international students or professionals working abroad; they meet their future husbands outside of the US military circuit. The Korean Inter-Married Women's Association (KIMWA) grew out of this historical shift. Lea Armstrong, a Tacoma resident who is a former KWA president and the founder and president of KIMWA, said, "This is a different era with different needs." Originating out of two international conferences in Seoul in 2004 and 2006, KIMWA has twenty-four local chapters in thirteen countries. Although KIMWA deals with longstanding issues like domestic abuse, it strives first and foremost to bring younger intermarried Korean women into contact with one another through social media, conferences, and leadership training.

Headquartered in Tacoma, KIMWA also helps to link multiracial Korean families in the Pacific Northwest with the rest of the world. The organization has expanded its constituency to include multiracial families in Korea. KIMWA offers Korean language classes for the non-Korean wives of Korean men and lobbies for constitutional provisions in Korea to prohibit racial and ethnic discrimination. It also sponsors scholarships and foreign exchange programs for multiracial residents of Korea. Some of these students have visited the Pacific Northwest as a result. By foregrounding multiracial Korean families, KIMWA has challenged and redefined what it means to be Korean. "As far as I'm concerned, every human being on this earth is mixed blood," Armstrong stated. "This whole world is already multi-ethnic, multi-cultural, multi-lingual. Accept them, it's a better world we're making." We are all poly-cultural.[11]

Toward a Korean American Politics?

Korean Americans, like all peoples, are difficult to categorize neatly. We span different generations. Some of us arrived in the United States very recently, while others have great-great-grandparents who landed in Hawai'i more than a century ago. Our political outlooks range from archconservatives to impassioned radicals. We are divided along the lines of gender, class, and sexuality. We are men

Members of the Morning Star Korean Cultural Center perform at a chuseok celebration organized by the Korean Inter-Married Women's Association of Seattle on October 10, 2011. Founded in 1985 and based in Western Washington, Morning Star is a traditional performing arts studio that performs around the world. Courtesy of Matthew Benuska.

and women, feminine and masculine, working poor and filthy rich, queer and straight. We are adopted, multiracial. Many of us have family back in Korea or elsewhere in the world. We are transnational. We are multilingual—English-speaking, Korean-speaking, Span-

---

11 Lea Armstrong, KAHS interview with Jessie Kindig, Tacoma, Washington, August 28, 2012; Tiffany Ran, "Korean Women Married to Non-Koreans Find Kindred Spirits at Local Conference," *Northwest Asian Weekly*, August 26, 2010.

ish-speaking. We are Christian, Buddhist, atheist. With so many differences among us, does it even make sense to talk about a common Korean American identity? Are our differences greater than our commonalities?

In spite of—or perhaps because of—our differences, Korean Americans have organized on multiple fronts to articulate a communal political identity. In 1993, a group of young Korean Americans began meeting once a month to create a social and professional network outside of Christian churches. The meetings evolved into the Korean American Professionals Society of Seattle (KAPS), which sought to link the Korean American community with the greater Seattle civic community. Around the same time, Korean Americans also organized the Korean American Voters Alliance (KAVA) to increase political participation and civic education within the Korean American immigrant community. KAVA, a non-partisan organization, ran successful mass voter registration drives that signed up four thousand new voters and sponsored candidates' forums before local elections. As KAVA expanded to reach across generations, younger Korean Americans began to assume leadership positions within the organization.

In 2006, KAVA became the Seattle chapter of the national Korean American Coalition (KAC), into which KAPS also merged in 2008. Founded by Korean Americans in Los Angeles in 1983 and now comprised of fifteen chapters across the United States, KAC has concentrated its work on civic education and community advocacy, notably during Sa-I-Gu in 1992. KAC-Washington, an all-volunteer nonprofit organization with nearly 4,500 members, hosts and coordinates a variety of activities—from high school mentorship programs and college career panels to happy hours and voter registration drives. KAC collaborates closely with other Korean American and Asian American organizations, including the Asian Pacific Islander Coalition, Korean American lawyers' and health professionals' associations, and immigrant rights groups.

Perhaps more than any other organization, KAC-WA strives to represent all Korean Americans. As a non-partisan political organization, it has tackled issues relevant to multiple generations, advocating for small business owners, raising funds for Korean studies at the University of Washington, and lobbying for accessible health care for immigrants and people of color. KAC-WA has been a visible force in May Day immigrant rights marches. Its multigenerational constituency sets the group apart, according to Shari Song, a cofounder of KAPS and past president of KAVA. "That's what makes it unique, that there's first and second generation on board. Older people, younger professionals, bilingual," she said. But it is a struggle to include everyone, to get more Korean Americans involved. That is KAC's mission and challenge, Song stated, because "we need to have more voices."[12]

In the meantime, individual Korean Americans have run successfully for political office and helped to make Korean Americans more visible to the larger society. Martha Choe

A volunteer helps to distribute the first Korean Language Voter's Guide, published by the Korean American Voters Alliance. Courtesy of the Korean American Coalition of Washington.

---

12 Shari Song, KAHS interview with Jessie Kindig (telephone), August 6, 2012.

rose to prominence as a member of the Seattle City Council in the 1990s. At the state level, Paull Shin became the first Korean American elected to the Washington State Legislature in 1992. Born in 1935 during the Japanese occupation of Korea, Shin personally experienced the deep costs of colonialism and war. After his mother died when he was a young child, his father abandoned him. When the Korean War erupted he was a homeless teenager. He found work as a "houseboy" for American military officers, one of whom adopted Shin after the war and brought him to the United States. After earning his Ph.D. at the UW, he taught East Asian studies at Shoreline Community College for about thirty years.

Shin never forgot his Korean and Asian American roots. After serving as Washington State's trade ambassador to South Korea, he was elected in 1992 to the Washington House of Representatives and in 1998 to the Washington State Senate, a post he held until January 2014. A Democrat from Edmonds, Shin has a constituency that is by no means limited to Korean Americans. He has nevertheless been a strong advocate for Korean Americans and Asian Americans. In 2002, he sponsored legislation to ban the use of the racially derogatory term "Orientals" in the state code. In 2007, he introduced a bill in the Senate to designate January 13 as "Korean American Day," to commemorate the day the first group of Koreans arrived in Hawai'i in 1903. Passed unanimously in both houses, Shin's bill was signed into law by the governor in April 2007. His career has inspired and influenced other Korean Americans to enter politics, including Cheryl Lee, Shari Song, and Cindy Ryu.[13]

In recent years, Cindy Ryu has become a leading Korean American politician in Washington State. Born in 1949 in South Korea, she grew up in a family struggling to adapt to a society ravaged by

---

13 "Honoring Paull Shin's Legacy for the State and Korean Americans," *Seattle Times*, January 16, 2014; Kim Johng Ho, KAHS interview with Chong Eun Ahn (telephone), September 8, 2012.

war. Her father worked as a migrant laborer in Southeast Asia, relocating his family to Brunei and the Philippines before moving to Seattle in 1969. Ryu eventually became a business owner before turning to politics. She steadily worked her way up the political ladder, winning election to Shoreline's city council and then the mayor's office in 2008. In 2010, Ryu was elected to the Washington House of Representatives. She was the first Korean American woman in US history to become a mayor and a state legislator.

Although Ryu has received widespread support from fellow Korean Americans, she grounds her politics in a broader vision of inclusiveness. She has worked on behalf of small businesses and public commerce, matters dear to many Korean Americans. Ryu was also one of the sponsors of a historic bill to legalize marriage for same-sex couples, which became law in February 2012. Though facing backlash from socially conservative Korean Americans for her support of that legislation, Ryu, a Democrat, is committed to advancing the rights and opportunities of marginalized peoples and communities. "I have this whole other background which a lot of other Americans can identify with, whether they came from Asia, or from Europe, or Africa, or South America," she said. "I have this whole plethora of support, as well as culture. I truly believe we can celebrate both being American, and in my case, being Korean, and pick the best of both worlds."[14]

In contrast to Shin, Ryu, and KAC-WA, a group of Korean American activists in and around Seattle has pursued issues not centered on civic engagement and electoral politics but on social justice. In 2006, when negotiations for the Free Trade Agreement (FTA) between South Korea and the United States were set to take place in Seattle, activists in Korea contacted Soya Jung and

---

14 Cindy Ryu, Biography, Washington State Legislature Website, http://www.housedemocrats.wa.gov/roster/rep-cindy-ryu/biography/; Cindy Ryu, "Reaching for the American Dream," video for the White House Initiative on Asians and Asian Americans, http://www.youtube.com/watch?v=7yH7YJyN-DEg.

Cindy Ryu with supporters during her 2014 campaign. Courtesy of Cindy Ryu.

Mijo Lee to help host and organize a week of protests against the FTA. The collaboration between Korean and Korean American activists—united in their objection to the FTA's promotion of multinational corporate interests above the struggles of ordinary workers and farmers—produced vibrant protests influenced by Korean political traditions. They included acts of civil disobedience and a *Sam-bo Il-bae* march down the streets of Seattle. If most Korean Americans in the Pacific Northwest did not join the protests, political organizing against the FTA pointed to new possibilities in defining Korean American politics.

Through the FTA protests and the alliance forged between South Korean and local activists on behalf of global justice, Jung and Lee recognized the need for a new kind of Korean American organization, one rooted in progressive activism. Though they had been involved in movements for racial justice for years, they realized that they had "just never really talked about being Korean." But the collaboration with Korean activists during the FTA protests and their previous work with Nodutol, a grassroots

Korean American organization based in New York City, inspired them to found Sahngnoksoo in Seattle in 2007. Sahngnoksoo— the Korean word for "evergreen," which represents strength, endurance, and determination—has focused most of its work on political education and discussion to generate a radical critique and an activist Korean American identity. They also aim to build political networks with progressive Korean Americans across the United States, Asian American organizations in Seattle, and Korean activists in Korea.

Far from trying to represent all Korean Americans, Sahngnoksoo's work seeks to reveal the historical contexts and political roots of the struggle to articulate a Korean American identity. It is a process that will inevitably produce tensions, contradictions, and debates among Korean Americans. Those alienated

Members of the Sahngnokosoo at the annual May Day March for Workers and Immigrant Rights in Seattle, May 1, 2008. Courtesy of Sahngnoksoo.

by Korean American churches and other mainstream Korean American organizations—notably adoptees and LGBT youth, among others—have especially gravitated to Sahngnoksoo. "We were surprised by how many people came and joined the organization," Jung recalled, "which really spoke to the fact that there was a need for something like that." The emergent community has begun working with other Asian American groups to address common issues like domestic and partner violence and sexual assault. "It goes with this shift in our mission to be more about being a resource for Korean activists," Lee explained. "What does it mean for us to be doing this kind of community accountability as Korean Americans, as part of an Asian American community?"[15] To one degree or another, that is a question that all Korean Americans are asking. In our daily lives and interactions, we are creating complex and contradictory answers.

---

15 Soya Jung and Mijo Lee, KAHS interview with Chong Eun Ahn and Jessic Kindig, Seattle, Washington, July 30, 2012.

CONCLUSION

What does it mean to be Korean American? If you ask that question to a dozen Korean Americans, you will likely receive a dozen different responses. It is, in effect, an impossible question. Rather than offer a definitive answer, what we have suggested throughout is that it is a question that cannot and should not be answered definitively. Instead, we invite our readers to think critically about how we conceive of and build our collective identities and communities. Claims or assumptions of an authentic or a definitive identity are inherently exclusionary. To give an example, at a Korean American church just north of Seattle not long ago, on an ordinary Sunday, a pastor chose to mock "American" efforts to extend equal rights to lesbians and gay men. To him, those efforts smacked of Western decadence that moved "Americans" (by which he was implying whites) further away from biblical teachings. Although he did not say so explicitly, this particular pastor was invoking a certain kind of Korean American identity and community, where those who transgressed sexual norms could find no home. In his mind, no one could identify as Korean American and LGBT.

What does it mean to be Korean American? We can surely approach that question in a way very different from that conservative pastor and in a way that does not merely acknowledge or celebrate our diversity. It is a question that we must struggle to answer as we move forward, not through silenced consensus but through critical exploration. A Korean American identity, like all identities, should not be viewed as something fixed, something given to us by our ancestors. As George Lipsitz puts it, "We do not choose our parents, but we do choose our politics."[1] And our identities and communities are fundamentally rooted in our politics, not in our genetic makeup. Arguments on cultural authenticity or inauthenticity will get us nowhere. Accusing fellow Korean Americans of not being

---

1 George Lipsitz, *The Possessive Investment in Whiteness: How White People Profit from Identity Politics* (Philadelphia: Temple University Press, 1998), viii.

"Korean" enough or being too "American" has no historical basis or intellectual merit.

Who are Korean Americans? We are a complex and heterogeneous people. We are a people shaped by *han*, a collective sense of suffering, oppression, and hardship. Yet, we are a people who survived, who struggled on. And if we are to survive as a people, we must forge identities and communities that reflect our history. We must continue to struggle—as Korean Americans, as Asian Americans, as human beings—for democracy and justice. "Injustice anywhere is a threat to justice everywhere," as Martin Luther King, Jr. said.[2] We cannot ignore, dismiss, or malign the most vulnerable among us—the poor, queer and transgender youth, battered women, undocumented workers. Attuned to our differences, to enduring hierarchies all around us, we can perhaps begin to imagine identities and communities that grapple with our varied and fractured histories to move toward a more just world. These aspirations are the ongoing legacies and contradictions of *han*. They should shape interpretations of our past and visions for our struggles ahead, in the upper left and beyond.

A pungmul team leads a protest against South Korean President Chun Doo Hwan in downtown Seattle, April 19, 1986. Courtesy of Dean Wong.

---

2 James Melvin Washington, ed., *A Testament of Hope: The Essential Writings of Martin Luther King, Jr.* (San Francisco: HarperSanFrancisco, 1991), 290.

Acknowledgments

Ick-Whan Lee, the visionary behind the Korean American Historical Society (KAHS), originally conceived this book project. He recruited Robert Hyung-chan Kim to inaugurate and direct the project, but some unanticipated turn of events forced Professor Kim to focus his energy on more pressing matters. Chong Eun Ahn and Jessie Kindig, graduate students at the University of Washington at the time, guided the project through the research stages. Kindig then wrote a preliminary draft of the entire book. Based on Kindig's draft, Moon-Ho Jung, the president of KAHS, completed the final draft. Matthew Benuska, the treasurer of KAHS, served as a consultant throughout and collected and organized all of the photographs.

Generous grants from the Overseas Koreans Foundation and additional financial support from the University of Washington funded our project. We also thank Joseph Hong and Hwasook Nam for offering their thoughts at various meetings and all of our interviewees for sharing their stories with us. Sun-Hee Yoon, Woonkyung Yeo, Chong Eun Ahn, and Nina Kim worked long hours to conduct, translate, and transcribe oral history interviews. Timothy A. Thomas collected and organized U.S. census records for the project.

Appendix
A Short List of Korean American Organizations

Asian Adult Adoptees of Washington:
http://www.aaawashington.org/wpress/

Association for Asian American Studies:
http://aaastudies.org/

Asian Pacific American Labor Alliance:
http://www.apalanet.org/

The Kidok News:
http://www.kidoknewsusa.com/

Korean American Association of Tacoma:
http://www.kaata.net/

Korean American Bar Association:
http://www.kaba-washington.org/

Korean American Coalition-WA:
http://kacwashington.org/

Korean American Grocers Association:
http://kagrowa.org/

Korean American Historical Society:
http://www.kahs.org/

Korean Inter-Married Women's Association:
http://world-kimwa.com/

Korean Women's Association:
http://www.kwacares.org/

Sahngnoksoo:
http://sahngnoksoo.wordpress.com/

Seattle-Washington State Korean Association
http://www.seattleka.org/

Seu Mi Sa Buddhist Temple:
http://cafe.daum.net/seumisa

United Seattle & Bellevue Korean School:
http://www.usbks.org/

University of Washington
American Ethnic Studies:
http://depts.washington.edu/aes/index.php
Center for Korea Studies:
http://jsis.washington.edu/korea/

Index